THE
ANXIETY
FIX

THE ANXIETY FIX

Text by Caitlin McAllister

An Hachette UK Company
www.hachette.co.uk

Vie Books, an imprint of Summersdale Publishers
Part of Octopus Publishing Group Limited
Carmelite House
50 Victoria Embankment
LONDON
EC4Y 0DZ
UK

www.summersdale.com

Printed and bound in Poland

ISBN: 978-1-83799-160-0

Substantial discounts on bulk quantities of Summersdale books are available to corporations, professional associations and other organizations. For details contact general enquiries: telephone: +44 (0) 1243 771107 or email: enquiries@summersdale.com.

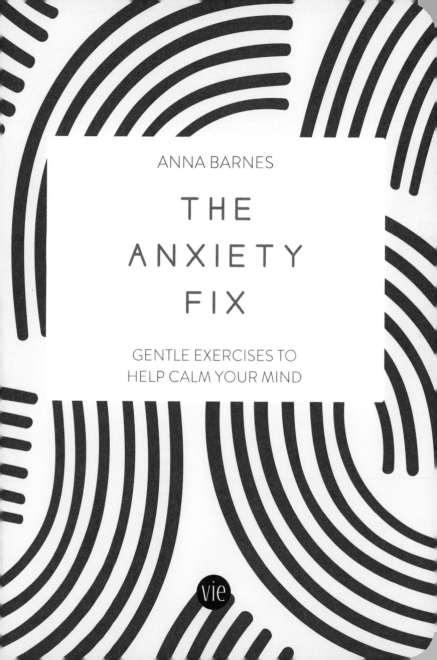

ANNA BARNES

THE
ANXIETY
FIX

GENTLE EXERCISES TO
HELP CALM YOUR MIND

vie

CONTENTS

Introduction	8
What This Book Will Do for You	10
How to Use This Book	11
Chapter 1: Anxiety and You	12
Chapter 2: How to Quieten Your Mind	46
Chapter 3: The Power of Self-Care	82
Chapter 4: Coping Strategies	118
Conclusion	154
Resources	155

INTRODUCTION

Has your anxiety been holding you back for far too long? If so, you're in the right place.

A little anxiety is normal for everyone, but it doesn't have to be a dark cloud over your life. *The Anxiety Fix* is designed to help you identify your triggers, interrupt the worry cycle before it spirals out of control, reframe negative thoughts, and calm your nervous system during life's stressful moments.

Any time your brain starts to run away with anxious, unhelpful thoughts, you can use this book as your very own box of tricks to steady your mind, relax your body, and bring your thoughts back to a neutral (or better yet, positive!) place.

The exercises in this book will prompt you to discover why you feel anxious, and how to acknowledge your emotions without letting them take over your day-to-day life.

With a mix of useful, research-backed advice, practical steps to instantly calm anxiety flare-ups, and fill-in exercises to help you address the underlying cause of your worries, *The Anxiety Fix* is your personal anxiety first-aid kit for when you need it most.

WHAT THIS BOOK WILL DO FOR YOU

This book can act as a circuit breaker for your anxious thoughts. When you're feeling worried or uneasy, it can provide you with useful exercises, anxiety-busting tools, and a gentle reminder that everyone feels this way at times.

No matter how permanent your anxiety might feel, you *can* take small steps to start feeling better instantly. When you begin to understand what anxiety actually is, the many different ways it can show up in your life, and the tried-and-tested coping strategies that will help you manage it day-to-day, you will start to feel a weight lift from your shoulders and your inner confidence return.

Greater well-being and living a happier, more fulfilling life are the goals, and this book will be the first stepping stone on your journey. By the last page, you will be closer to feeling less burdened by anxious thoughts, enjoy more mental clarity in daily life, and be able to swap panic for peace at any given moment.

HOW TO USE THIS BOOK

This book is for you if...

- You feel like you're being held back by anxious thoughts
- You aren't sure what triggers your anxiety
- You would like to exercise your self-belief and self-esteem
- You want to practise self-care to maintain positive mental health
- You want to start working towards your biggest life goals free from worry
- You want to create your own bank of resources to draw from in stressful situations.

If anxiety is a big obstacle for you, and is getting in the way of living the life you want, you'll find that this book offers a blend of holistic advice, practical tips and thought-provoking exercises to help you create real, lasting change. *The Anxiety Fix* is your step-by-step guide to addressing the root cause of your worries.

From helpful daily trackers to identify where your anxiety comes from, to mindful breathing that can be utilized during stressful episodes, the tips and exercises in this book are designed for a variety of scenarios. You can spend an evening with some, and just a few minutes with others, so give some thought to whether you will work through them day by day, or apply them when anxiety next rears its head. It is best to work through the pages of this book one by one, but you may also benefit from revisiting certain exercises later if you find them particularly helpful. The book is designed to be read at your own pace, allowing you to dip in and out whenever you are ready to tackle an anxious thought.

CHAPTER 1:

ANXIETY

AND YOU

You have probably felt it before: thoughts seem to whirl around your mind at the speed of light, your heart starts thumping, your stomach churns, your mouth gets dry, your palms become sweaty, your breathing speeds up, and you can't focus on anything else.

This is anxiety.

Maybe you feel all of these symptoms when something stressful happens to you. Maybe you feel just one of them. Or perhaps your worries show themselves in another way. Anxiety is our mind and body's reaction to stress, and this is a normal part of the human experience, but it doesn't have to limit us in daily life.

Anxiety looks completely different for everyone, so in this chapter, you will learn why anxiety happens to you, how it appears in your life, what your triggers are, how your mind and body are connected, and how – in many situations – you can actually *use* anxiety to your advantage.

WHAT IS ANXIETY?

Anxiety can take many forms. It is usually experienced as a general feeling of uneasiness or worry, and this can be mild, or, in some cases, severe and debilitating. We all feel the occasional bout of anxiety as we go through life – when preparing for a presentation at work or going into a school exam, for example. This is normal, and it would be strange if we didn't feel a little anxious during life's big moments.

However, if you feel anxious on a regular basis or find it difficult to keep worries under control, this can start to have a negative impact on your daily life. Anxiety is one of the most common mental health issues and is nothing to be ashamed of, but it is something you can take steps to improve in order to feel calmer.

If you believe you suffer from a more serious anxiety disorder, you may wish to see a doctor or medical professional who can support you by recommending an appropriate treatment. Or, if you live with a low level of anxiety, some resources (like this book) could help you learn more about your anxiety and start to feel better.

ANXIETY OR WORRY: WHICH IS IT?

Do you ever wonder if what you are experiencing is anxiety, or just an everyday "brain cloud"?

A brain cloud is a temporary state of overthinking that afflicts everyone from time to time, and it's usually attached to a specific upcoming event or decision. Brain clouds tend to come and go relatively quickly, passing like the clouds in the sky. Anxiety, on the other hand, may arise regardless of what is going on in your life, and could cause significant unease. It could even impact your daily functioning.

With anxiety, you might experience mental symptoms such as feeling nervous or tense, feeling you're in danger, or being unable to control your rumination. You may also experience physical symptoms such as an increased heart rate, rapid breathing or trouble sleeping.

Here are a few features that may help you distinguish between anxiety and brain clouds:

Brain cloud	Anxiety
• Happens every so often • Occurs before a stressful event or decision • You can usually distract yourself from the feeling • You spend a fair amount of time thinking about an upcoming event • You might voice your concerns to loved ones	• Happens regularly • May not be connected to a specific event or decision • You find it difficult to distract yourself from the feeling • You think about it constantly • You might experience physical symptoms or signs • You may not feel comfortable telling others how you feel

WHY DOES ANXIETY EXIST?

Anxiety may feel like a huge nuisance, but there is actually a very good reason for it being part of life.

Believe it or not, we were *designed* to feel anxious. Throughout human history, anxiety has served a purpose: when there is danger around, our bodies prepare to take action by sharpening and increasing some of our physiological functions, such as our heart rate, breathing and – perhaps most frustratingly – our thoughts.

Anxiety is the body's way of alerting us to possible threats.

On an average day, we might not often encounter situations that trigger our fear response, but our anxiety response can kick in much more easily – even when there is no physical threat and we are not in a life-or-death situation.

Nowadays, anxiety is more commonly the body's way of telling us we are uncomfortable. The brain tends to mistake the potential for failure, or a slight inconvenience, for real danger.

Historically, our anxiety might have been triggered when we realized we didn't have enough food to stay alive. In our modern world, it might become triggered when we think we won't get a parking space. Learning how to manage feelings of anxiety when they arise, no matter the situation, can be an incredibly useful life skill.

HOW COMMON IS ANXIETY?

Anxiety is one of the most common mental health conditions in the world, affecting an estimated 4.05 per cent of the global population according to the World Health Organization.[1] Even those who are not diagnosed with an anxiety disorder will experience it from time to time, and that's totally normal.

Problems tend to arise when your anxiety goes from occasional, mild and related to a particular event or decision, to constant, intense and not related to anything significant.

Although anxiety is common, this does not mean that you need to live with it on a day-to-day basis, especially if it is affecting your happiness, relationships, career, life goals or something else in a negative way.

By recognizing when your anxiety arises, *why* it arises, and finding the best tools to bring yourself back to a state of peace (like the ones you'll learn later in this book), you can start to treat anxiety like an untrained dog. Right now it's jumping and barking when someone rings the doorbell, but if you give it a little love and some firm instruction, it will learn to stay alert but calm when something new comes knocking.

THINGS THAT TRIGGER ANXIETY
(FROM THE INSIDE)

Many people believe that their anxiety comes out of nowhere, with no underlying cause or reason behind it, but, as we are discovering, this is typically not the case. Even if you feel your anxiety build from nothing, if you dig a little deeper you can usually find an origin event or fear that is causing these feelings.

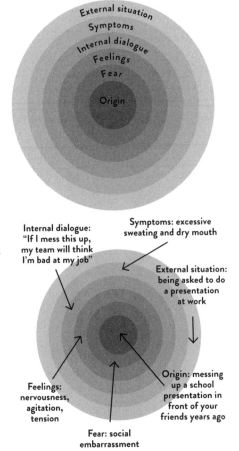

External situation
Symptoms
Internal dialogue
Feelings
Fear
Origin

The origin of anxiety is often closely related to our deepest insecurities and how we see ourselves. Underlying fears will usually dictate our feelings, what our mind tells us, the physical symptoms we experience, and our response to an external situation. For example:

Internal dialogue: "If I mess this up, my team will think I'm bad at my job"

Symptoms: excessive sweating and dry mouth

External situation: being asked to do a presentation at work

Origin: messing up a school presentation in front of your friends years ago

Feelings: nervousness, agitation, tension

Fear: social embarrassment

THINGS THAT CAUSE ANXIETY
(FROM THE OUTSIDE)

There are many external circumstances or events that can prompt anxiety. Some things are small and quickly subdued, while others are more persistent or scary, and therefore difficult to tackle.

Always remember that everyone's circumstances are unique, and we each have a different threshold at which we start to experience stress. Read through these examples and see if any are familiar to you:

Parenting challenges

Going on a date

Sitting an exam

Driving a car somewhere new

Travelling to a different country

Going to the doctor

Attending a party or gathering of friends

Flying on a plane

Being apart from a loved one

Not achieving at work

Not fulfilling a life goal by a certain age

Having too much in your social calendar

There are lots of underlying reasons why you may experience anxiety, and you may feel it coming on in very specific, seemingly meaningless, situations. That's OK. No matter what is behind your worries, the tools in this book can help.

THINGS THAT CAUSE *YOUR* ANXIETY

Now it's time to think about where *your own* anxiety originates. You can go as deep as you like here. Think about what might have happened in the past, who in your life might have influenced your worries, and what untruths your mind tends to tell you in internal dialogue.

You may wish to use these prompt questions:

External situation: What are you doing when anxiety strikes?

Symptoms: What physical and emotional symptoms come up?

Internal dialogue: What is your brain telling you? Any questions or comments?

Feelings: What feelings do you start to notice?

Fear: Underneath your worries, what is there a fear of?

Origin: Why do you fear this so much? What might have happened in the past to make you feel this way?

Now fill in your own and see what you can discover about yourself:

External situation:

Symptoms:

Internal dialogue:

Feelings:

Fear:

Origin:

THE MIND-BODY CONNECTION

When we experience stress, we can develop unexplained physical symptoms alongside our mental worries. Studies have found that anxiety can cause physical reactions like sweating, shortness of breath, trouble sleeping, dizziness, restlessness, muscle aches and more.[2]

Remember that we are designed to react this way, and although it can be frustrating when the body does things we don't want it to, these physical reactions can be useful indicators that it's time to take steps to quieten the mind. There are many calming techniques mentioned later in this book, but knowing when to implement them begins with acknowledging the physical symptoms and tapping into what's really behind them.

There is an undeniable connection between the mind and the body, so the next time you feel strange physical symptoms before you give a presentation in front of 100 people or socialize with a group of friends, take them as signs that your mind is trying to tell you something.

HOW ANXIETY SHOWS UP IN THE BODY

The next time you feel anxious, use this page to tap into your physical symptoms and to figure out where in your body anxiety is showing up, and how. Is it an emotion? A physical pain? An uncomfortable feeling?

Sometimes it can be hard to put the anxiety experience into words, but acknowledging that something feels different in your mind and body can help you move through the feeling with more intention and ease.

Try this: Find a safe place to sit, clear your mind and tune into your body. Here are some prompts that might help you do this:

- Pick a word to describe how your body feels right now.
- Have you noticed any changes in your body since the anxiety began?
- Where in your body do you feel the most tension?
- Does your anxiety feel more like physical pain, discomfort or something else?
- If your anxiety was a colour, what colour would it be?
- If your anxiety was a shape, what shape would it be?
- If your anxiety was a person, what kind of personality would they have?

As you ponder the above, jot down some of your thoughts or doodles here:

WHAT ANXIETY LOOKS LIKE

Anxiety can show itself in a number of ways. Here are a few examples of how anxiety might show up physically in our bodies. You can use the empty boxes to note down your own examples – what does anxiety do to *your* body?

Biting your
fingernails

Rapid breathing

Sweating and/or
clammy hands

A rapid
heartbeat

Redness on your
face and/or neck

Wide eyes/a
worried look

Tapping nervously
or pacing

WHERE IS YOUR ANXIETY?

If you have an episode of anxiety, write down any feelings or physical symptoms that apply to each area of your body. You can use the diagram below to do this. Labelling every section of the body is not necessary, but consider each part carefully and try to tune into where you feel the most discomfort.

WHAT ANXIETY SOUNDS LIKE

As well as those external physical signs, anxiety often shows up in the mind, almost like a voice in our heads. Here are some examples of what it might be telling us (even if there is no evidence to suggest that it's true). You can use the empty boxes to fill in your own – what does anxiety sound like to *you*?

"The worst-case scenario is likely to happen"

"People around me can tell how I'm feeling"

"What I said in the meeting yesterday will get me fired"

"This date has to go well or I will be alone forever"

"My blood test results are going to reveal something sinister"

"Everyone at this party is judging my outfit"

"I'm going to fail at the presentation and everyone in my class will laugh"

Separating yourself from your anxiety by thinking about what it looks and sounds like can help remove its power. By imagining it as its own separate being, instead of a part of you, you start to realize **you are not your anxiety**.

HELLO, MY NAME IS ANXIETY

Let's give your anxiety a face! Close your eyes, take a deep breath, and imagine what your anxiety might look like. Is it shaped like a human? Like an animal? Does it have any distinguishing features? Does it seem angry? Friendly? Is it so big it towers over the building you're in? Or is it so small you need a magnifying glass to see it?

There are no wrong answers! Just as you might draw a monster as a child, use the space below to doodle what you think your anxiety looks like.

WORRY
OFTEN GIVES
A SMALL THING A
BIG SHADOW.

_____

Swedish proverb

ANXIETY TRACKER

Tracking your anxiety can help you identify when it comes up most often, and what might trigger it. Over the next few days, answer the following prompts each time you experience an anxiety flare-up. If you can, answer the prompts as soon as possible, either while you are feeling anxious or immediately after the anxiety has dissipated, so the feelings are fresh in your mind.

Anxiety flare-up 1

What day and time is it?

Is anything significant happening right now?

What physical symptoms are you experiencing?

What feelings are you having?

What internal dialogue is going on?

Can you identify the origin of this anxiety?

Anxiety flare-up 2

What day and time is it?

Is anything significant happening right now?

What physical symptoms are you experiencing?

What feelings are you having?

What internal dialogue is going on?

Can you identify the origin of this anxiety?

Remember, no one needs to see these pages but you, so be honest about what is making you feel anxious. Later in this book you will learn solutions to tackle your anxiety, but for now, you just need to recognize the feelings and sit with them.

BRAIN vs REALITY

Our brains have a habit of lying to us, especially when anxiety is at play. When we are anxious, our brains will think up ways to convince us that negative things are true. For example, if someone with social anxiety is hesitant to attend a party, their brain will do everything to convince them that attending is not a good idea.

Here are some things it might say vs what the reality is likely to be.

Brain	Reality
"I won't know anyone there."	You know at least one person there, otherwise you wouldn't have been invited.
"No one will talk to me and I'll feel lonely all night."	If no one talks to you, talk to them. A simple "How do you know the host?" will kick-start the conversation.
"Everyone will judge my outfit."	Most people will be too focused on their own outfit to pay attention to yours.
"I'm not good at making small talk."	You are only half responsible for the conversations you have, which means others need to make an effort with you too.
"I'm going to be anxious all night and not enjoy myself."	You could meet your new best friend at the party. There are so many possibilities that it could end up being one of the best nights of your life!

Remember, you can't trust anxious thoughts because they are often defeatist. Each time your brain tells you that something negative will happen, balance it out by thinking of something positive that could happen instead. Later in this book you will learn more ways in which to identify and interrupt negative thoughts.

ANXIETY TRIGGERS

Anxiety almost always has a root cause, or something at the centre of the worry and fear that's causing someone to feel the way they do. Everyone has their own unique anxiety triggers that cause these flare-ups. These could be big things like:

- A build-up of work or exam stress that leads to eventual burnout
- A big life change such as a house move or a loved one in hospital
- Losing a job or source of income, or getting into debt

Anxiety can also be triggered by small, seemingly insignificant things such as:

- An off-the-cuff comment from a work colleague about your performance
- Not being able to fit into an outfit you once did
- Bickering within your family or friendship group

We all have different triggers when it comes to anxiety, and what might rattle one person's state of mind might barely affect someone else.

Remember: If you feel that you can't discuss your anxieties because other people's worries seem more legitimate, relevant and "real", know that this is not the case. Whether your anxiety is caused by a big life event or something that seems of minor importance, appreciate that your reasons for feeling the way you do are valid. You are always allowed to acknowledge how you feel, no matter the cause.

YOUR ANXIETY TRIGGERS

Use the prompts below to fill in what you have learned about your anxiety triggers.

My anxiety is triggered most when

When this happens, I feel

I know that underneath my anxiety is a fear of

HOW MUCH ANXIETY IS TOO MUCH?

A little anxiety in response to an external trigger is normal and happens to us all. But when is it considered *too much* anxiety? At what point does it start to cause real problems in daily life? Is it overwhelming your every thought and feeling? The scale set out below might help you determine where your anxiety sits.

- I'm so anxious I can barely leave the house. It is affecting my work, relationships and other areas of my life. I regularly feel that something awful is going to happen.

- My anxiety overwhelms every thought I have and is deeply affecting my relationships with loved ones.

- My anxiety is always present at a high level. It regularly keeps me up at night and affects my relationships.

- My anxiety is always present at a low-to-medium level, and I have trouble relaxing.

- Before big events/decisions, I worry a lot and it keeps me from truly experiencing things because I am distracted.

- I worry quite a bit, but only before big events/decisions.

- I get the occasional anxious thought that passes on its own.

If you are on the low end of the scale, you may be able to manage daily life without much trouble but could benefit from understanding more about how to use anxiety to your advantage. If you are on the high end of the scale, don't worry. You may be significantly impacted by anxious thoughts, but the tools in this book can offer a first step to better understanding yourself and to calming the chaos in your mind.

HOW ANXIETY CAN BE HELPFUL

Anxiety is a lot of things: annoying, frustrating, debilitating, depressing... helpful?

Yes, anxiety *can* actually be a useful tool. In an earlier section, "Why Does Anxiety Exist?", we discussed how anxiety is an evolutionary tactic for keeping us safe. Both fear and anxiety do this by causing a physical reaction or a feeling that prompts us to take action:

Fear can often trigger a physical response, such as grabbing a railing to stop ourselves from falling.

Anxiety is a feeling that might alert us to a loved one being close to potential harm.

So how can anxiety be helpful? Well, it's a feeling that the brain utilizes whenever there is something to worry about. It kicks us into gear and encourages us to figure out how to fix the situation.

In the second scenario above, anxiety is designed to ring alarm bells in the brain that tell us "If you don't take action now, your loved one might come to harm."

HOW TO USE ANXIETY IN MODERN LIFE

Anxiety can be useful in today's world. Here are a few ways in which we can harness anxiety in daily life and use it to our advantage:

If you are attending a social event, thank your anxiety for trying to save you from an embarrassing situation, and let it know you'll be absolutely fine. Your anxiety can give you the burst of energy you need to get through the evening.

Before a presentation at work, let your anxiety spur you on to perfect your slides and run over your speech. Anxiety just wants you to do well, so use it as fuel to practise.

If you get anxious as a parent, it means you are alert, aware and always ready to step in if your child does something potentially dangerous. While it might not feel nice (and it's OK to want to do something about it), a small amount of parental anxiety is normal and helps to keep little ones safe.

Before a date, remember you only feel this way because you care about making a good first impression. The other person is probably feeling the same, so your anxiety could calm theirs and put them at ease.

When your bank account is getting low and you feel anxious about money, use this feeling as motivation to get your finances in order.

HOW DOES ANXIETY HELP YOU?

Now it's time for you to make friends with your anxiety. Even if you hate the feeling, chances are your anxiety wants to keep you safe in some way. Fill out the prompts below to find out more about your anxiety and its purpose...

I get most anxious when   and my anxiety

shows itself with physical signs like

and thoughts of

I think my anxiety does this because it wants to keep me safe from

Instead of hating it, from now on I will tell myself

DEAR ANXIETY...

By treating your anxiety as a worried friend who wants to keep you safe, you can start to change your negative opinion about it. In the space below, write a thank-you letter to your anxiety. Think about all the times it has helped you out by providing useful gut feelings, encouraging you to prepare for important things, and keeping you safe from real danger.

Dear Anxiety...

HOW TO MAKE FRIENDS
WITH YOUR ANXIETY

As already said, your anxiety is there to help you avoid dangers, failures, embarrassments, and more. Often, we must override the feeling in order to continue doing things anyway, regardless of our underlying fears and worries.

The reality is that anxiety is a part of you, as it is for everyone, and it won't go away completely. No matter how much therapy or self-growth work we do, we can only learn to control our anxiety, not get rid of it entirely – and this is not a bad thing.

Just as you wrote a thank-you letter to your anxiety, write a script for yourself for the next time anxiety flares up. Tell it that you plan to feel the fear and do it anyway. Use these prompts or feel free to write your own from scratch.

"Thanks for your input, Anxiety. I appreciate that you want me to

avoid   by making

me feel   ,

but I want to   ,

so I'm going to do this anyway. I know I'm going to be OK."

ANXIETY AND SLEEP

Picture it. You are cosy in bed trying to get to sleep, and suddenly, as if from nowhere, a question pops into your head:

"Did I send that email I was supposed to send today?"

You think about it for a while, decide you can't do anything about it right now, and close your eyes again. But something called the Worry Cycle kicks in:

"What if I didn't send it? Will my boss be angry tomorrow? Will they lose a client because of this email? If they do, will they fire me? If I get fired, would I need to give up my house?"

These thoughts continue on and on until any possibility of sleep is long gone. According to the Sleep Foundation, sleep disturbances such as insomnia have been associated with anxiety disorders for many years, and as you probably already know, this can cause a vicious cycle.[3]

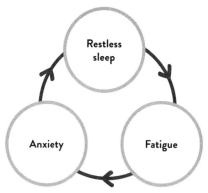

Not only will working on your anxiety make you feel better day-to-day, but it could also help you at night. If you struggle to sleep because thoughts keep swirling around your mind, try the exercise on the next page to clear your head before bed.

THE EVENING BRAIN DUMP

A "brain dump" is a little like a brainstorm, except that instead of thinking of ideas, you think of all the things that are cluttering up your mind. This page can be a super-useful tool to empty any anxious thoughts from your head before you try to sleep. By recording them elsewhere, it gives your brain permission to release them and, hopefully, get a little more slumber.

Use the space below for your Evening Brain Dump.

Do you feel lighter already? You may want to make this part of your nightly routine.

ANXIETY AND RELATIONSHIPS

Our personal fears and anxieties can hold us back, which, over time, can start to affect our relationships. Remember that while anxiety is a very personal experience, it can affect the people around you as well.

Here are some of the ways anxiety can negatively affect relationships:

- If anxiety stops you from doing certain things, it may also stop your loved ones from doing them, which could become a source of resentment.
- When anxiety makes you preoccupied because you are ruminating, you may act differently, forget things, and not really listen to people.
- Anxiety can cause you to be pessimistic, grumpy or even short-tempered. While this is not a problem in the short term, it can be off-putting to others if it lasts.
- Anxiety in parenthood can mean that your children don't get to have certain experiences because you believe they are dangerous.
- A romantic partner may feel they need to take care of you, help you cope, and regularly change plans because of your anxiety, which can be a lot to take on.
- People in your life may need to be aware of, and avoid, your anxiety triggers, which could then cause anxiety for them as they don't want to upset you.

Taking steps to address your anxiety and learning how to handle it day-to-day can strengthen your relationships, as the people in your life get to experience the best version of you.

RELATIONSHIP CHECK-UP

Take time to journal about how your anxiety could be managed to improve your relationships with others, and how the people in your life might feel as a result. You may also want to jot down what positive changes *you* could experience in your relationships as a result of addressing your anxiety.

ANXIETY
AND HEALTH

As we now know, anxiety can lead to physical symptoms as well as emotional ones, but it goes even further than this. Prolonged anxiety, especially if it is severe, has been linked to health conditions such as high blood pressure, heart disease, irritable bowel syndrome (IBS), a weakened immune system, and more.[4]

Not only is addressing anxiety helpful for making you feel better in yourself, but it could be vital to your long-term health and wellness. Here are some examples of simple things you can do to maintain good physical health while addressing your underlying anxiety:

- Start walking more and increasing your daily step count.
- Eat a balanced diet that excludes excess sugar, salt and processed foods.
- Move your body throughout the day, especially if you have a sedentary job.
- Drink plenty of water.
- Supplement with any vitamins and minerals that your diet lacks.
- Start a regular exercise routine, like jogging, swimming or yoga (even once a week is a great start).
- Prioritize and take steps to improve your quality of sleep.

HEALTH CHECK-UP

Take a minute for a quick health check-up. Do you have any physical ailments that you believe could be related to your anxiety? Think back to pages 21 and 22 and mentally scan your body, see what comes up, and note them here. Even if they are not related to your anxiety, noting them down so you can start to address them could be a huge weight off your mind.

SUMMARY: ANXIETY AND YOU

You will now have a much better understanding of anxiety and how it relates to you. This chapter included a deep dive into:

- What anxiety is, where it comes from and how it could be affecting your life
- The mind–body connection and how anxiety might be showing up physically in your body
- What anxiety looks like, sounds like and feels like for others and for you
- When anxiety is likely to show up in your life, and in what form
- How to use anxiety to your advantage
- How anxiety affects each area of your life in the long term, and what to do about it.

Remember that you can use the exercises in this chapter again and again for any other anxious thoughts that come up. You may also want to recreate the Anxiety Tracker pages in a separate notebook to further explore when, how and where anxiety is present in your life.

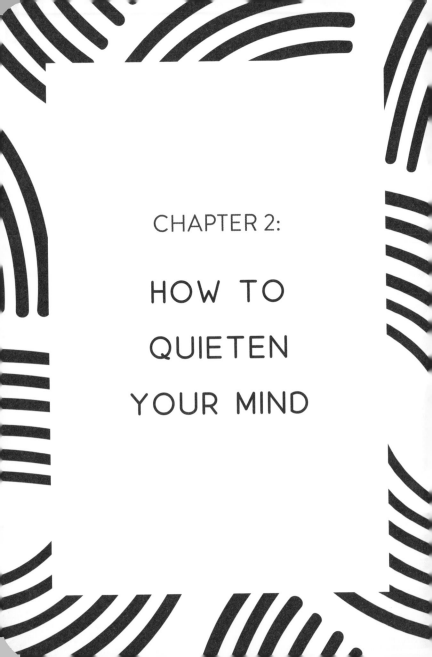

CHAPTER 2:

HOW TO
QUIETEN
YOUR MIND

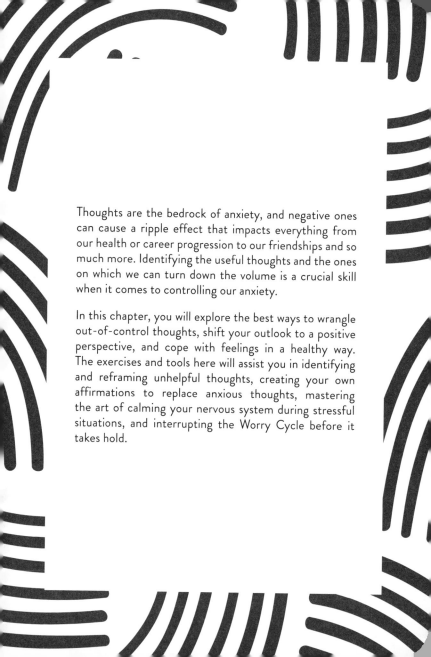

Thoughts are the bedrock of anxiety, and negative ones can cause a ripple effect that impacts everything from our health or career progression to our friendships and so much more. Identifying the useful thoughts and the ones on which we can turn down the volume is a crucial skill when it comes to controlling our anxiety.

In this chapter, you will explore the best ways to wrangle out-of-control thoughts, shift your outlook to a positive perspective, and cope with feelings in a healthy way. The exercises and tools here will assist you in identifying and reframing unhelpful thoughts, creating your own affirmations to replace anxious thoughts, mastering the art of calming your nervous system during stressful situations, and interrupting the Worry Cycle before it takes hold.

ANXIETY IS A
PASSING CLOUD
AND I KNOW
THE SUN WILL BREAK
THROUGH SOON

THE LOUD MIND

Do you ever feel like your brain overheats due to excessive thinking? As humans have evolved, we have slowly begun to increase the number of things we need to think about each day.

In the past, we may have thought "What berries will I forage for dinner?" or "Where can I find shelter?" Now, it sounds more like "How do I do my taxes?", "What shall I buy my mum for her birthday?", "How do I get promoted at work?" or "Which baby formula has the best ingredients?" and so on. It's no wonder our brains feel overwhelmingly loud at times.

With so much to think about, sometimes anxious thoughts become louder than the rest in order to be heard above the chatter in our heads. Acknowledging that we may have a little too much going on in life, not enough downtime to recharge, and that not everything can be a priority all at once, can really help to bring us back to a base level of noise.

We must find ways to quieten anxious thoughts until we are ready to take action on them.

~~SILENCE~~ QUIETEN YOUR MIND

Anxiety has a bad habit of taking a tiny whisper of a thought and amplifying it. Thoughts get louder in our minds until we find ourselves ruminating on something that has happened in the past or hasn't happened at all yet.

You may feel that your worries are all-consuming, spiralling out of control, and are so intrusive that they interfere with daily life. It may also feel impossible to shut them out of your mind entirely, but luckily you don't have to create a mental dam to hold them at bay.

Instead of completely silencing your anxious thoughts, it can be more useful to find practical ways to make them quieter and less overwhelming. You can do this by acknowledging your worries for what they are (helpful thoughts that are just trying to keep you safe), interrupting the cycle of worry before it has a chance to spin out of control, and incorporating some helpful activities into your daily routine to keep the noise down.

THE TRAJECTORY OF A THOUGHT

The trajectory of a positive thought is similar to that of a negative thought, except both can land in very different places when it comes to our emotions. A thought can lead to a feeling, which can lead to an action, which can lead to a specific outcome. Here is an example of what this might look like in real life:

Thought: "I'm great at my job"

Feeling: Confidence at work

Action: Preparing well for a big presentation

Outcome: A promotion

Now let's see what could happen with a negative thought:

Thought: "I'm awful at my job"

Feeling: Anxiety when discussing your ideas with colleagues

Action: Shying away from opportunities to challenge yourself at work

Outcome: Never progressing from your current role

Thoughts have so much power, both positive and negative. By stopping negative thoughts in their tracks and reframing them as positive ones we change the trajectory of their outcome, and, as a result, we can change the trajectory of our lives in powerful ways.

THE WORRY CYCLE

When we come up against something stressful or start to ruminate on things that we lack control over, the Worry Cycle kicks in. What begins as a harmless thought can take on a life of its own as worries compound. Eventually, a feeling of overwhelm sets in.

Below you can see the Worry Cycle in action.

TRIGGER
You get an email about an upcoming meeting.

WORRY
You imagine the things that could go wrong in the meeting, such as turning up late, forgetting a document, or saying the wrong thing to your boss.

PHYSICAL SYMPTOMS
Your body prepares itself for action by engaging different bodily functions; your heart beats faster, and you start to feel a little nauseous.

CATASTROPHIZING
As your physical symptoms become more intense, your mind starts to imagine the worst: "Is this meeting just for me? Am I being fired from my job?"

NEW WORRY CYCLE BEGINS
The possibility of being fired begins a new cycle of worrying about other things, for example, being fired could mean being unable to pay your mortgage.

BREAKING THE WORRY CYCLE

Now, bring to mind a situation that reliably gives you anxiety. This could be a one-off event, like taking an international flight, or something that you encounter on a regular basis, like certain social interactions. Fill in the cycle below with your thoughts.

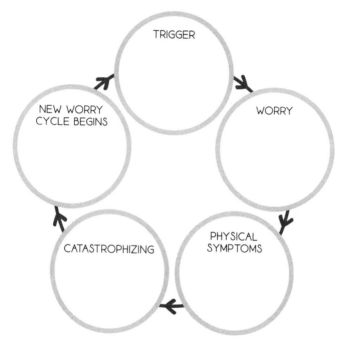

It is not realistic to go through life avoiding our triggers entirely, but we can learn to interrupt the Worry Cycle by reframing negative thoughts with positive ones at the worry stage – an anxiety fix that can help you avoid the physical symptoms, stop catastrophizing, and put an end to the Worry Cycle until next time.

LABELLING THOUGHTS

Anxious thoughts can feel big, intense and all-consuming when they are happening and we can mistake them for the truth. To make them less absolute, one of the best things we can do is to label them as negative thoughts. For example:

"I'm going to do badly in this exam"

becomes...

"I am having the negative thought that I'm going to do badly in this exam."

This is a minor change, but in the second example we become more distanced and detached from the thought. By labelling them as exactly what they are – just thoughts! – we see that they are not necessarily the truth, and we can separate them from real life.

Once you get the hang of labelling anxious thoughts as potentially negative thoughts, you can go a step further and turn them into positive ones:

"I am having the negative thought that I'm going to do badly in this exam, but I've studied hard, and I'm prepared, so I know I'm going to do my best."

IDENTIFYING AND REFRAMING NEGATIVE THOUGHTS

Identifying and labelling negative thoughts as they happen can offer an opportunity to interject with a positive one instead. With a little practice this becomes easier over time. Here are some examples of negative thoughts and how you could reframe them:

Type of thought	Example	Reframe
All-or-nothing thinking	"I've never been invited to any of her parties, so she must not like me."	"I've never been invited to any of her parties, but that seems fair since she doesn't really know me that well."
Focusing only on the negatives	"We always lose to this team. Our last win was a fluke."	"We won our last game. We can do it again today!"
Mind reading	"She rearranged our date to next week, so she's not interested in me."	"She rearranged our date to next week instead of cancelling it, so she must want to see me again."
Fortune telling/ predicting a negative outcome	"It's no use. I know I'm going to fail the test."	"I'm not sure how this test will go but I can only try my best."
Catastrophizing	"I was so awful in the talent show. It couldn't have gone worse."	"I'm not happy with my performance at the talent show, but people still cheered for me, so I can't have been that bad!"

This takes practice, but after a while you will start to recognize these thoughts as they happen and flip them on their head straight away.

FIND YOUR ANXIOUS THOUGHTS

Imagine your weekly schedule. Do you go to work Monday to Friday? Do you take the kids to ballet classes on Wednesday nights? Do you dog-sit for your friend every second Thursday? Go to brunch on a Sunday morning? Use the schedule below to create an overview of a typical week, find where your anxious thoughts are hiding, and label and reframe them, just like you did in the previous pages. Here's an example:

What's on?	Is anything stressful?	Label the anxious thought	Reframe the anxious thought
Morning meeting Work 9 a.m.–3 p.m. Pick up the kids Book club.	Monday meetings make me wish I'd prepared more in advance.	I'm having the feeling that Monday meetings are stressful.	I'm having the feeling that Monday meetings are stressful, but I know everyone feels the same pressure, and I'm not doing less than anyone else in the room.

Now it's your turn:

	What's on?	Is anything stressful?	Label the anxious thought	Reframe the anxious thought
MON				
TUES				
WED				
THUR				
FRI				
SAT				
SUN				

HOW TO TAKE CONTROL
OF YOUR THOUGHTS

... and stop them taking control of you.

If we don't intervene by labelling and reframing negative thoughts soon after they arise, they can take on a life of their own. What starts as one innocent negative thought can become our entire personality if we allow it to.

If you're thinking "I can't do that. I always forget to stop my negative thoughts and reframe them," then the thought is beginning to define you. Use what you have learned on the previous pages to reframe this assumption about yourself.

Here are three simple ways to remind yourself to label and reframe thoughts in the moment:

- If you tend to get negative thoughts about your self-image, stick a reminder Post-it on your mirror.
- If your negative thoughts come when you're at social gatherings, set an alarm on your phone for halfway through the evening. No one else will know what it means, but you'll be reminded to turn any negative thoughts around then and there.
- If you get negative thoughts while driving, record yourself saying positive affirmations and play this during your journey, to remind you to reframe anything negative.

Remember, your thoughts don't have to control you. You control them, so don't give up on reframing negative thoughts if you forget the first few times. Eventually you will get the hang of it.

DISTRACT YOUR NERVOUS SYSTEM

In the moment, anxiety can feel all-consuming. Your heart might be racing, your breath might be shallow, your body might start sweating. These are all physical signs that your autonomic nervous system has kicked in, which is your fight or flight response.[5] This biological mechanism is designed to prepare you to defend yourself against danger or run away. Great if you're being chased by a predator, not so great if you're trying to complete an everyday task!

Instead of allowing your nervous system to continue in overdrive, a distraction can do wonders for restoring a sense of calm. This might be something as simple as going for a walk, or you might need to learn some therapy-based techniques to add to your toolkit for future anxiety flare-ups.

Remember, there are positive distractions – like the ones you'll read about in the next few pages – and negative distractions. Negative distractions might include things like alcohol, reaching for unhealthy snacks that tend to upset your stomach, or calling a friend who always leaves you feeling bad about yourself.

Although negative distractions might make you feel better in the short term, they're likely to make you feel worse further down the line. Make the negative distractions less readily available for when anxiety strikes next and opt for positive distractions instead.

MEDITATE

Meditation is regularly touted as a must-try for positive mental health, and it certainly has some benefits for those who suffer from anxiety. Meditation comes in many forms, but at its core is the practice of focusing your thoughts in one specific area. When your mind wanders, you don't judge it, you simply pull it back to the present moment over and over again until it becomes easier to focus on the now. Meditation is regularly recommended for those with anxiety and stress issues, and it's a free, easily accessible tool you can use anywhere.

You will find thousands of guided meditation videos online, but if you are completely new to the practice, start small by finding a quiet, comfortable place in your home, setting a 5-minute timer, and closing your eyes.

Know that in the beginning your thoughts will undoubtedly wander towards whatever anxieties you're currently experiencing, and that's OK. Try not to judge yourself or get frustrated. Gently guide them back to the present moment.

Some people like to think of these thoughts as clouds passing, so imagine them drifting into your mind and then the wind carrying them straight back out.

BREATHE

You may have tried meditation and decided that it isn't for you, but remember that meditation takes many forms, and with a little more exploration you could discover a mindfulness activity that does work for you. This might be walking meditation (where you remain mindful while taking slow, deliberate steps on a walk), yoga (where you stretch your body into various poses while focusing on the present moment), or breath-focused meditation.

Breathwork encompasses a variety of breathing techniques to help you stay focused on the present moment while affecting the body's nervous system. There are a number of different types, but all use a series of breathing patterns to help you achieve an optimum state. With regular, safe practice, this could immediately have a positive impact on your anxiety.

Exercise:

One easy breathwork technique that can help to reduce anxiety in moments of high stress is Box Breathing. This breathing cycle requires you to:

- Inhale for 4 seconds
- Hold your breath in for 4 seconds
- Exhale for 4 seconds
- Hold your lungs empty for 4 seconds
- Repeat until you begin to feel your anxiety dissipate.

JOURNAL

Journalling is regularly used in therapy as a tool to process thoughts and feelings, and you have already used a few journalling techniques in this book.

Often our minds are a jumble of emotions, ideas, memories, hopes, dreams, worries and a million other things. It can be exhausting to hold it all inside! If feeling overwhelmed is contributing to your anxiety, then regular journalling could be an excellent activity for you to try – all you need is a pen and paper.

The thing to keep in mind when you start journalling is that no one ever needs to see what you write down (and you can throw away the page when you've finished if you prefer). You should be as honest and thorough as you can so that your brain can purge itself of all the anxious thoughts it is holding on to and so begin to process them. You should also remember that your journal entry *does not need to be perfect*. Make it messy. Make it nonsensical. Just get your thoughts onto the page!

After a while you might find that by writing things down, you naturally give them structure, meaning and a conclusion. What was once a hurricane of anxious thoughts whirling around in your brain can turn into an eloquent journal entry with a solution at the end.

_____'S JOURNAL

Journalling is a wonderful tool for anxiety that can be accessed easily at any time. Use the space below to write in. You might want to use a prompt (there are three here to get you started), or feel free to jump straight in with whatever you feel would help you most.

1. What's making you anxious this week?

2. Describe your perfect, anxiety-free day.

3. What could you take action on this week that would make you feel better?

NOTHING DIMINISHES ANXIETY FASTER THAN ACTION.

Walter Anderson

GET SOME EXERCISE

Taking measures against anxiety doesn't always mean physical action, but one way to get out of a rut and reduce your anxiety quickly is to exercise. Many studies have found that physical activity can help significantly reduce the symptoms of anxiety,[6] and although we don't always feel like it, getting off the sofa and moving around can be a great way to distract our minds and boost our endorphins.[7]

Moving your body doesn't need to mean vigorous exercise. Breaking a sweat can certainly help, but so too can these gentle movement ideas, which can also kick anxiety to the curb:

- Take a brisk walk in nature
- Do gentle yoga or some simple stretches at your desk
- Do arm exercises with some light weights while you watch TV
- Cycle to work once a week
- Start swimming a few lengths of your local pool

SWITCH OFF FROM SOCIAL MEDIA

Social media can be both a positive and negative influence on our mental health. While it is a great resource for keeping in touch with friends and family, the negative effects of overusing it have become more and more apparent in recent years.

Studies have suggested that prolonged use of social media platforms may be related to symptoms of anxiety and other mental health concerns, particularly in young people. It can add to an information overload and the pressure to compare ourselves to others, and can even cause us to fixate on how others view us, so limiting your use is often a simple way to start addressing the problem.

Even if you don't believe that social media is an issue for you, doing a few days of social media detox could help quieten anxious thoughts and diminish worries. The easiest way to do this is to remove the apps from your phone so that you aren't tempted to check them out of boredom or habit.

Other ways to switch off from social media include installing app timers that limit your usage, putting your phone in a drawer while working, and enjoying social media-free Sundays to recharge your mental batteries.

GET PERSPECTIVE
FROM SOMEONE ELSE

When anxiety has clouded our thoughts for so long, it can be difficult to see the wood for the trees, so discussing your worries with a trusted friend or family member could bring things back into focus and help you figure out what's in front of you.

Getting someone else's perspective on an issue can be invaluable. It quickly unburdens your brain, allows you to say the issue out loud for the first time, and gives you access to possible solutions you may not have thought of. Remember that everyone has had a different upbringing and life experience, so just because you can't think of the best solution doesn't mean that someone else won't be able to. And even if they can't, they may well make you feel better in the short term.

If you're embarrassed or feel awkward about telling someone your worries, you could send a message instead, or perhaps go for a walk so that your chat isn't the main focus.

CHANGE YOUR ENVIRONMENT

Have you ever wondered why people feel so much more relaxed when they come back from a holiday? Yes, they've had time away from work, but they've also had time away from their life. It's easy to become caught up in the mundane everyday routine, and to care a little too much about things that don't seem to matter much when we've had some time away. If anxiety is getting to you, it may be that you're feeling uninspired and in need of a change of scenery.

You don't need to go away on holiday to do this. You could go on a day out to somewhere you've never been before, visit an attraction you've always wanted to tick off your bucket list, or just go for lunch with a friend to get away from it all for an afternoon. Even a few hours away from whatever is causing your anxiety can help give your mind a breather and encourage it to start thinking of solutions on its own.

ZOOM OUT

Just as a change of scenery can help refresh our positivity, so can taking a glimpse at the bigger picture. When the Worry Cycle takes over it allows tiny, insignificant things to grow in the mind until mild anxiety becomes severe. A small thing such as the FOR SALE sign next door grows into a clear image of living next to a raucous family with a noisy dog and seven children who kick footballs near your windows. Would this be an ideal scenario? No. Would it be the end of the world as you know it? Also no.

Whenever an anxiety-inducing situation occurs, try to imagine the perspective of a drone camera hovering above you. Imagine it flying up further until it is hovering over your home; higher and higher until it can see your whole street; and then higher still until it can see the town or city you live in. Take note of how you feel: do your anxieties seem as bad from this vantage point?

This exercise can help you to forget about the issues that loom large in your mind and to see life from a new perspective. With a bird's-eye view, everything seems smaller, less obtrusive and more manageable.

COMMIT TO POSITIVE SELF-TALK

Anxiety often uses negative self-talk to make us feel bad about ourselves, and that we are not mentally equipped to handle certain situations. You might recognize negative self-talk as:

"I can't do anything right"

"I look so scruffy today"

"I'm bound to screw this up"

Remember that learning to catch those negative comments (even if they're only in your mind) is crucial to improving your anxiety. Your thoughts become your feelings, so thoughts such as these are likely to leave you feeling foolish, sad, worried and defeated.

Here are some examples of positive self-talk that, with a little practice and commitment, you can make stick:

"I'm really good at this"

"I'm looking and feeling great today"

"I love trying new things – let's see if I'm good at this!"

GRATITUDE

"Gratitude practice" is emerging as another tool for both shrinking anxiety and replacing it with positive thoughts. Research suggests that gratitude – the act of being thankful for the things you have – could have a positive impact on mental health.[8]

Gratitude can redirect the mind away from anxious thoughts, help to ground you, keep you in the present moment, and reduce rumination, all while triggering the release of neurotransmitters like serotonin – the happy hormone!

It is also beneficial because it encourages us to look at the bigger picture and be grateful for everything in our lives, rather than focusing on small, insignificant concerns – and this helps us, ultimately, to navigate future challenges.

Here are a few ways in which you could begin to practise gratitude:

- Every night before bed, think of three things you are grateful for that day.
- Send someone you love a message of appreciation.
- Associate something common in your day with gratitude (for example, every time you walk through a doorway).
- Each time you spend quality time with loved ones, message them afterwards to tell them how much you enjoyed yourself.
- If you catch yourself complaining, follow up your statement with "but at least…" and find something positive to be grateful for.

_____'S GRATITUDE JOURNAL

Feeling grateful already? Write it down! You can use the next two pages to journal some things you're grateful for in your life. Remember, these can be as huge as being grateful for the roof over your head, or as tiny as being grateful for discovering an extra biscuit in the bottom of the box you thought was finished. Anything goes!

74

AVOID YOUR BAD HABITS

For some people, turning down the volume on their anxieties may mean ignoring the call to engage with bad habits. We all have them: drinking too much caffeine, sleeping in late, procrastinating, hanging out with people who don't have our best interests at heart – the list goes on. Our bad habits hold us back from becoming the person we want to be, and the more we succumb to them, the further we get from the life we want.

For many of us, anxieties arise from the guilt caused by bad habits, so addressing these first can be a helpful way to quieten anxiety. Here are the steps to tackling bad habits:

1. Identify them. You may not even be aware of your habits, so write out a weekly planner and track when your bad habits come up.

2. Identify and remove your triggers. Often bad habits begin with a trigger, so identify yours and change them so that they become less accessible. For example, if you watch too much TV, remove the television set from your bedroom.

3. Replace your bad habit with a good one. Create a trigger that leads to a positive habit. For example, if you want to learn a new language, put flash cards next to your toothbrush so you can read them while brushing your teeth.

4. Get an accountability partner. It can be easier to break a bad habit with the help of a friend. Enlist someone who can provide positive encouragement.

USE AFFIRMATIONS

Affirmations are a powerful tool. In time, affirmations can become prominent in your mind, ready to defend against negative thoughts before they creep in, and this can have a positive impact on your mental health.

Here are some examples of positive affirmations you could say to yourself in the morning:

"Today is going to be an amazing day."

"Everyone is going to see how confident I am today."

"I'm a capable person."

"I am calm and prepared for anything life throws my way."

"Anxiety doesn't faze me. It comes and goes quickly."

"I've got all the knowledge and experience I need to make today great."

"I am in control of my thoughts at all times."

START A CREATIVE PROJECT

Want to quieten your anxious thoughts quickly? Sink your teeth into a project. While distracting yourself isn't a long-term strategy for tackling anxiety, it can be a good way to ease tension and restore some calm. A creative project using your hands is a great way to do this.

Here are a few creative projects that might inspire you to start your own:

- Paint a self-portrait of you happy and carefree
- Write a poem about overcoming anxiety
- Make a photo collage of all your favourite places
- Start a blog about something you're passionate about
- Make a vision board for your dream life
- Learn an instrument and write a song about happiness
- Make a piece of furniture from scratch that will make you proud every day
- Knit something for yourself to wear
- Make handmade gifts for your friends' birthdays

Whatever it is you have always wanted to try, set up an area at home where you can carry out your creative pursuit and go there any time you feel anxious.

LIES ANXIETY TELLS US

Anxiety can be pretty hard on us, but the golden rule about anxiety is that having a thought doesn't make it true. During those times when you're feeling particularly anxious, think about what anxiety is claiming you can't do, and list out all the reasons why that's not true. For example:

Anxiety: "I'm not going to get this job because I'm not qualified enough, and they'll probably hire internally."

Reasons why that may not be true:

1. If they weren't open to external candidates, they wouldn't be advertising the job.

2. I have just as much chance as anyone else.

3. They liked me enough to invite me to an interview, so they must see promise.

4. There is nothing to say I won't make a great impression when I meet them.

5. I know I can do this job well.

6. Experience and education aren't always essential if they believe I will work hard.

7. Thinking I won't get the job is just a thought; it's natural to feel nervous. I'll give it my best shot.

YOU *CAN* DO IT

We can strip anxiety of its power by not believing its negative assumptions about us. What do you get most anxious about each week? Dig deep to find your self-confidence, and list all the reasons why you're more than capable enough to handle it.

-
-
-
-
-
-
-

SUMMARY: HOW TO QUIETEN YOUR ANXIETY

You will now have a set of skills that enable you to take control of your anxiety before it gets a chance to take control of you. This chapter included a deep dive into:

- How thoughts work, both positive and negative, and how to properly label them
- How to reframe negative thoughts before they grow in our minds
- The Worry Cycle and how we can interrupt it with useful, mindful activities
- Journalling and how to use it to manage our mental health
- Why simple things like switching off from social media and saying morning affirmations can help us turn our life around
- The power of gratitude and positive thinking

There are so many useful tools in this chapter for when you create your Anxiety First-Aid Kit (more on this later!) so take a note of your favourites to come back to.

I CAN TURN DOWN THE
VOLUME ON MY ANXIOUS
THOUGHTS AT ANY TIME.
BETTER STILL, I CAN
CHANGE THE CHANNEL.

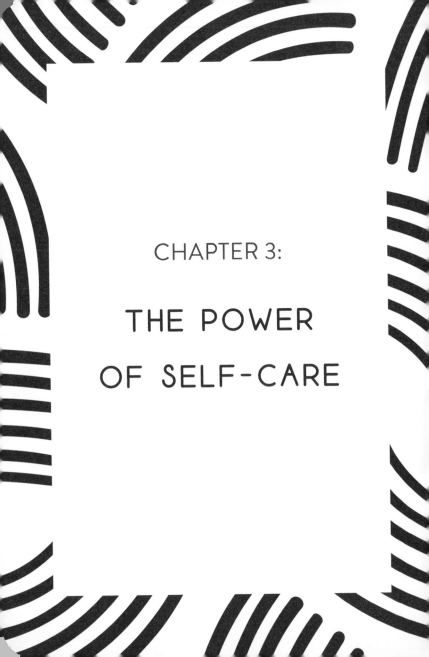

CHAPTER 3:

THE POWER
OF SELF-CARE

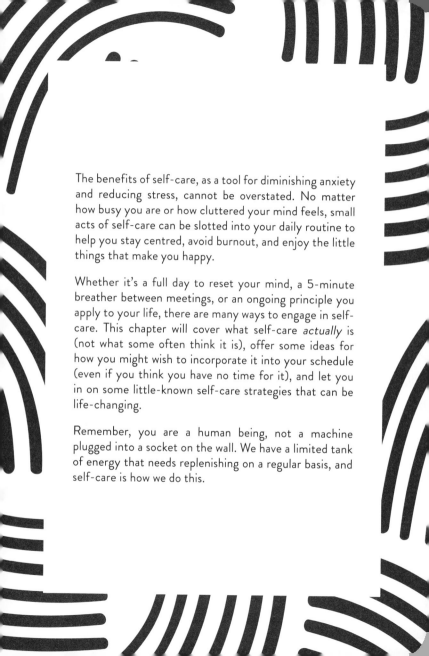

The benefits of self-care, as a tool for diminishing anxiety and reducing stress, cannot be overstated. No matter how busy you are or how cluttered your mind feels, small acts of self-care can be slotted into your daily routine to help you stay centred, avoid burnout, and enjoy the little things that make you happy.

Whether it's a full day to reset your mind, a 5-minute breather between meetings, or an ongoing principle you apply to your life, there are many ways to engage in self-care. This chapter will cover what self-care *actually* is (not what some often think it is), offer some ideas for how you might wish to incorporate it into your schedule (even if you think you have no time for it), and let you in on some little-known self-care strategies that can be life-changing.

Remember, you are a human being, not a machine plugged into a socket on the wall. We have a limited tank of energy that needs replenishing on a regular basis, and self-care is how we do this.

WHAT IS SELF-CARE AND WHY IS IT RELEVANT TO ANXIETY?

When anxiety starts to rain on your parade, think of self-care as the umbrella that can be whipped out to keep you dry until the weather clears. Although self-care has largely been thought of as relating to physical health, the definition has become broader in recent years, and today anything that is helpful in taking care of your physical, emotional and mental health would be considered self-care.

If you experience anxiety symptoms, self-care can be useful in the following ways:

- It tends to make us feel good physically and mentally
- It can help distract you from what is worrying you
- It can bring your attention back to your body
- It helps you focus on what you *need*, rather than what your anxiety wants
- It acts as a release valve when stress builds up

Self-care might relate to physical wellness, such as booking a long overdue doctor's appointment, or it might be an act of mental wellness, such as meditating for 15 minutes each morning. Tap into what you need and make time to engage in some self-care.

BEWARE OF THE
BUBBLE BATH FALLACY

When you think of self-care, you may conjure up an image of someone soaking in a bubble bath with a book, or with a mug of tea in their hand. For a long time this kind of self-care has been held up as the pinnacle of wellness. But is it really? A bubble bath can be enjoyable, wellness-boosting, and indeed blissful, but don't get caught in the trap of believing that it is the bath itself that holds the power.

At its core, wellness doesn't come from the warm water or the fancy bath bomb, it comes from those 10 minutes of silence; 10 minutes to yourself; 10 minutes to let your mind wander to new things; 10 minutes to come up with a solution to whatever your problems are, and so much more.

The Bubble Bath Fallacy isn't just about bubble baths, it is the mistaken belief that something surface-level and superficial that may make us feel good for a few moments is actually an act of self-care. Instead of getting distracted with having the latest aromatherapy oil (one that promises to boost your energy), it is far better to discover what you actually need.

If you need more energy, don't buy a crystal; rest.

If you need a little silence, don't go on a three-day silent meditation retreat; go for a walk.

If you need more connection in your life, don't join a networking group; reach out to a friend.

Find the REAL act of self-care that will serve you best.

TREAT YOURSELF WITH KINDNESS

A big part of self-care is self-kindness, but so many of us treat the people in our lives with much more kindness than we do ourselves.

Scenario 1: Your friend is anxious about an upcoming work trip where she must present her ideas to a board of directors. You send a text message the week prior to see how her preparations are going. You call her the night before to say "You've got this! You've worked SO hard and you're going to seriously impress with your ideas. They'll be blown away by your brilliance!" When she's done you send flowers and a card that says "Congratulations! Take some time off now and celebrate what you have achieved."

Scenario 2: You're anxious about an upcoming work trip where you must present your ideas to a board of directors. The week before, you rip up a bunch of your ideas because you're certain they're not good enough. The night before, you can't sleep, thinking "I haven't worked hard enough on this, and they're going to hate all my ideas." When it's over, you spend the next week reliving all the little things that went wrong.

Do you see the difference in how we tend to treat ourselves versus how we would treat the people we love? The next time you feel anxious, try to think about the pep talk you might give to a friend. You deserve exactly the same love and care.

HAVE SELF-COMPASSION WHEN YOU MAKE MISTAKES

Just as we should learn self-kindness, we should also be better at self-compassion. When a child makes a mistake, we don't automatically berate them for it and tell them how silly they've been. We're much more likely to tell them that everything will be OK and then gently guide them in the right direction for next time.

For many people, anxiety comes from the fear of making a mistake, so learning to be compassionate to ourselves when we do make mistakes is a valuable skill. Compassion not only makes us feel better in the short term but could also positively impact our long-term anxiety by stopping us from ruminating on our mistakes. With practice, we begin to learn that it's OK to make mistakes and that we don't need to be quite so anxious next time.

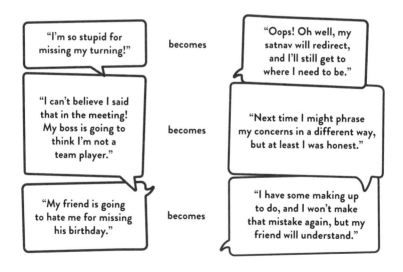

"I'm so stupid for missing my turning!" *becomes* "Oops! Oh well, my satnav will redirect, and I'll still get to where I need to be."

"I can't believe I said that in the meeting! My boss is going to think I'm not a team player." *becomes* "Next time I might phrase my concerns in a different way, but at least I was honest."

"My friend is going to hate me for missing his birthday." *becomes* "I have some making up to do, and I won't make that mistake again, but my friend will understand."

PHYSICAL SELF-CARE FOR THE MIND–BODY CONNECTION

Although self-care should be thought of as a holistic activity that encompasses physical, emotional and mental health, focusing on the physical side of things can provide a lot of benefits. If you aren't sure what will make you feel better mentally, then starting with physical self-care can have a positive knock-on effect.

By looking after yourself outwardly, your inner self will begin to feel the benefits too.

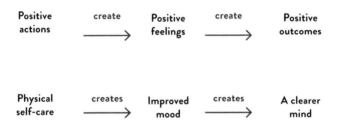

| Positive actions | create → | Positive feelings | create → | Positive outcomes |
| Physical self-care | creates → | Improved mood | creates → | A clearer mind |

Physical self-care can also provide a tangible tool for feeling better and wrangling any out-of-control anxiety. While we may not feel like addressing the underlying emotions connected to our anxiety, it may be easier and more accessible to go for a swim, eat a healthy meal or do a breathwork exercise, or whatever activity tends to give you an immediate boost.

The significance of the mind–body connection is huge, so by starting with some external, physical self-care steps, we can eventually start to reap the benefits internally too.

EAT WELL AND STAY HYDRATED

When we are super-anxious and have a lot on our minds, sometimes the last thing we want is to be told to eat a healthy meal and drink some water. We tend to reach for quick, easy meals when we are stressed, like microwaveable snacks and takeaways. However, maintaining a balanced diet that cuts down on processed, sugary or overly salty foods can have a significant impact on our anxiety. In fact, studies have found that a healthy diet that meets nutrition recommendations, can help to reduce symptoms of anxiety.[9]

When you eat and drink well you feel healthier. Changing your diet and drinking more water won't necessarily cure your anxiety, but doing so can be a foundational habit that can contribute to a less anxious mind that can more easily bounce back to its calm self. Eating a balanced diet and drinking enough water won't happen unless you plan to live a healthier lifestyle.

Everyone's idea of "healthy" is different, so don't think about what you should be doing based on all the wellness tips on social media. Instead, plan out some meals for the week ahead that are healthier than the ones you had the week before. When you have completed this, you can work on making the week after even healthier.

WEEKLY FOOD PLANNER

Use this table to plan out your healthy meals for the next week.

	Breakfast	Lunch	Dinner	Snacks
MON				
TUES				
WED				
THUR				
FRI				
SAT				
SUN				

MOVE YOUR BODY

One of the best self-care activities you can do to instantly boost your mood and distract from anxious thoughts is to move your body. This doesn't need to mean vigorous exercise or even breaking a sweat. Some gentle movements with purpose can do the trick.

Low-impact activities such as swimming, yoga or going for a long walk can make you feel better quickly. Exercising puts the focus on the body rather than what is going on in the mind, and also releases feel-good endorphins to naturally elevate mood.

Here are a few ways you can start to move your body more in day-to-day life:

- Do seated yoga at your desk to stretch and relieve any stiffness
- Take your dog for a walk, and get your heart rate up by throwing a stick for them to fetch
- Take the stairs any time you have a chance instead of using the lift
- Walk to or from your university classes instead of taking public transport
- Cycle to work instead of taking the car
- Make catch-ups with friends more active by choosing an exercise activity to do together
- Put on music and dance while doing your housework to make the chore more fun and energetic

While anxiety tends to make us feel like we're helpless and at the mercy of our brains, exercising can offer a feeling of being in control of your body and mind once again.

EXERCISE PLANNER

Use the table below to plan out your exercises for the week. Keep in mind that you do not need to do a big, sweaty workout every day. Choose some activities that are easy to incorporate into your week. For example, Tuesday could be "Ask the team to do a walking meeting instead of sitting in the conference room," and Saturday could be "Take the stairs instead of the lift when I visit John's flat."

	Today's exercise	How do you feel as a result?
MON		
TUES		
WED		
THUR		
FRI		
SAT		
SUN		

REST AND SLEEP

Getting an adequate amount of rest plays an important part in managing anxiety, which, if left to its own devices, can disturb sleep. Research suggests that anxiety can have a negative impact on REM (rapid eye movement) sleep, as shown below.

The brain uses sleep to process emotions and memories, and a lack of sleep can affect the neurotransmitters needed to do this, making us less resilient to external stressors. If sleep eludes you, here are a few things you can do to give yourself the best chance at catching those Zs:

- Maintain a consistent bedtime and wake-up schedule to regulate your body clock.
- Remove distractions from your bedroom and optimize it for sleep by making it quiet, dark and cool.
- Create a bedtime wind-down routine, such as reading a book, or breathing deeply.
- Have a warm bath or shower. Boosting circulation to your skin and extremities helps cool your core body temperature, enabling you to fall asleep quicker.
- Consider how your body reacts to caffeine and reduce your intake if necessary.
- Do not look at screens before bed. Social media stimulates the brain and makes us want to keep scrolling, plus the screen light can disrupt sleep-inducing hormones.

WEEKLY SLEEP TRACKER

Use the table below to note how much sleep you had each night and how you feel as a result.

	How much sleep did you have last night?	Rate your anxiety from 1 to 5 1 = Low 5 = High	What one thing can you do to improve your sleep tonight?
MON			
TUES			
WED			
THUR			
FRI			
SAT			
SUN			

SPEND TIME OUTDOORS

One of the easiest ways to banish anxiety quickly is to step outside your front door. That's it! Spending time outdoors has so many benefits for those looking to improve their anxiety symptoms. Being in nature (particularly green spaces) has been found to promote relaxation, reduce stress, and trigger the release of endorphins that help to enhance mood and relieve anxiety.

There are a number of reasons for this: we get exposure to sunlight, which gives us a healthy boost of vitamin D, and we engage our body by walking, running or playing, which helps us decrease any tension we're holding on to. In fact, healthcare professionals now recommend "nature-based health interventions" that encourage people to take part in nature-based experiences to improve their health and wellness.[10]

Whether you're going on a rigorous hike up a mountain or just sitting in your back garden with a cup of tea, spending time outside can provide a whole host of wellness benefits.

MAKE TIME FOR PEOPLE
WHO MAKE YOU FEEL GOOD

Anxiety often involves other people. Whether this relates to your relationship insecurities, your colleagues creating a stressful work environment, or to something else, anxiety can be caused or made worse by the people around us, whether they mean to or not. How we choose to engage with others is entirely up to us.

No one can control the actions of other people, however we can limit our anxiety by focusing primarily on our closest, most important relationships.

Spending time with people who lift you up with their positive attitude is likely to alleviate some of your anxiety. Spending time with those who drain your energy, engage in gossip, burden you with their problems and always talk about themselves is likely to increase it.

Think about people in your life who encourage you, make you feel good, offer emotional support, and ease your anxious thoughts. Lean into these relationships by making more time for them and enjoy the feeling of having a solid support network around you.

If someone in your life is a negative influence and increases your anxiety, spend less time with them. You may not be able to (or want to) cut them out of your life completely, but you can set boundaries around how much time you spend with them and how their comments affect you.

CURRENT DAILY SELF-CARE SCHEDULE

Use this weekly planner to write down what you typically do throughout the week, and where you fit in any self-care activities. You will have the chance to write down the self-care activities you would *like* to be doing on the next page, but here, focus on what you currently do, and don't worry if you can't think of much.

	Morning	Afternoon	Evening
MON			
TUES			
WED			
THUR			
FRI			
SAT			
SUN			

How does the above planner look to you? Do you think you do enough self-care each week? Do you think a general lack of self-care could be contributing to your anxious feelings? Think about this before you fill in the next page.

IDEAL DAILY SELF-CARE SCHEDULE

Now, use this weekly planner to write down what your dream week of self-care would look like. Where could you find little pockets of time for activities that will recharge your batteries? Be realistic, but optimistic.

	Morning	Afternoon	Evening
MON			
TUES			
WED			
THUR			
FRI			
SAT			
SUN			

How does the above planner look to you? Have you managed to find time for the things you love doing, and the things that replenish your energy stores? You may wish to go to your own daily calendar or scheduling tool and add a few of these in to see if you can make them happen in real life.

BOUNDARIES ARE SELF-CARE

Setting boundaries may not seem like an essential part of self-care and anxiety management, but it could be one of the most important changes you make. Our relationships with loved ones and acquaintances can be wonderful, uplifting, positive things, but they can also be draining, challenging and frustrating at times. We all have responsibilities and commitments to others, but we shouldn't need to bend over backwards to fulfil them, nor should we need to let them affect our mental health and well-being.

That's where setting boundaries comes in, and – before you shy away from the idea – setting boundaries will not make people dislike you.

Setting boundaries might involve communicating your needs to people in your life, respecting your own time more, and saying no to things you don't want to do.

It's OK if you don't know your boundaries yet. From now on, for each request that comes your way, try to take a few seconds before jumping in with your answer. Think about whether it will make you overwhelmed or stressed. Think about what your priorities might be. And think about whether or not the activity in question will ultimately nurture your mental health.

YOU MAY NOT
CONTROL ALL THE
EVENTS THAT HAPPEN
TO YOU, BUT YOU CAN
DECIDE NOT TO BE
REDUCED BY THEM.

Maya Angelou

HOW TO SET HEALTHY BOUNDARIES

If you need some boundary-setting inspiration, here are some things you could try:

- Put your phone in a drawer until midday, or until you feel ready to look at messages.
- Say no to social events that are likely to leave you feeling depleted. You don't need to make up excuses or explain – a simple "I won't be able to make it" will do.
- Add your personal "opening hours" and response time to your email signature so people know when to expect a reply.
- Be honest with your manager at work if you feel you have too much to do. Consider the phrasing when you bring this up. "I feel I could be even more productive if I delegate more" could be effective as it conveys that you want to make the team as efficient as possible.
- Tell your friends if their words are hurtful or are making you feel stressed. You could say something like "I know you don't get along with Michael, but he's a good friend of mine, so I'd like to avoid talking about him as it makes me uncomfortable."

Remember, doing any of the above won't make people dislike you if you tell them about your boundaries in a direct yet friendly way.

YOUR BOUNDARIES

You may be starting to think about what some of your own boundaries are. Perhaps you already have some and didn't quite realize it, or maybe you feel there is room to implement a few more in order to alleviate some of your anxiety. Use the mind map below to brainstorm some boundaries you might want to set in each area of your life. Some examples have been added for inspiration:

Work	• Make it known that I will reply to emails once in the morning and once in the evening • •
Romantic relationship	• Tell my partner that they are now responsible for buying birthday presents for their side of the family • •
Social life	• Ask Sally to meet at the coffee shop nearer my house this time because I am always the one to travel far • •
Family	• Let my family know that we prefer they call before popping over so we can be prepared for company • •
Home	• Tell my teenage children that I won't be tidying their room for them any more • •

FOCUS ON YOU

Anxiety tends to come from worrying about what's going on around you, and what other people are doing, thinking or feeling. It can be both selfless and self-centred at the same time. For example, if you worry endlessly about whether or not someone enjoyed your dinner party, you are thinking about how you are perceived, while simultaneously thinking about whether or not you effectively met the needs of your guests.

Instead of asking yourself "Did they have a good time at the dinner?", reframe this to ask, "Did I have a good time at the dinner?" This is not self-centred, it is simply disregarding the things you can't change (whether or not your guests had fun) and refocusing on your own feelings and enjoyment.

This reframing tool can be used in a number of scenarios to bring the focus back to you and the only things you can control.

Anxious thought	Reframe
"Did the interviewer think I was a good fit for the job?"	"Is the place a good fit for me, and did I like the team?"
"Did I bring enough snacks to the school bake-off? Were they popular?"	"I got some great recipes from the other parents. I can't wait to try them."
"I'm worried my date didn't find my jokes funny and won't call."	"I probably won't call because I don't think our sense of humour matches."

DO SOMETHING GOOD

Focusing on yourself for a change, instead of on the needs of others, can be helpful. However, if you want an instant happiness boost (great for your self-care!) then doing something nice for someone else could also help.

Research has found that doing positive things for others can make you feel good as a result and could leave you feeling more fulfilled than if you did something nice for yourself. Here are some examples of things you could do to help others:[11]

- Send a card to a long-distance friend to say you're thinking of them and value their friendship
- Donate some money to charity
- Ask an elderly neighbour if they need any groceries
- Bring some tasty snacks into the office to share with your colleagues
- Organize a big day out with your whole family
- Reach out to a friend who has a lot on their plate, and offer to help with something
- Give your dog the best day ever with an outing to the park, their favourite treats, and lots of belly rubs
- Volunteer for a cause that means a lot to you
- Pop in for a cup of tea and a chat with someone who lives alone
- Join the clean-up crew in your local green space to help the environment

MAKE YOUR OWN JOY

It's far too easy to let anxiety rule our minds and to wait for external sources to grant us validation. Fretting over whether or not you'll be invited to your friend's birthday party, worrying that your podcast will never really take off, or being concerned that you won't find "the one" before you turn a certain age – all of these things rely on other people's input. It's time to make your own joy, regardless of what other people say, do or think.

If you're anxious about whether or not you'll be invited to your friend's birthday party, accept that you may not be, and that's OK. Book to do something fun on that day instead.

If you're worried that your podcast listenership isn't growing, focus on rediscovering the joy in recording, even if your podcast never becomes any more popular than it is now.

If you're concerned that you won't find "the one" any time soon, list out all the other things in life that bring you joy, and lean into those things instead.

Remember: we can't control what happens to us, or what doesn't, but we can control how we respond either way.

CREATIVE SELF-CARE

Have you ever got so into a creative project that you've completely lost track of time? Have you even, perhaps, lost hours while in the flow state?

Self-care can be found in the things we love to do, the things that bring us joy and that allow us to express ourselves. A little creative self-care can help us to shut off our brains for a while and focus on making something we're proud of. There are so many ways to engage in creative self-care (you'll find some ideas on page 77), but let's take photography as an example. You could:

- Try taking photos that capture your anxious thoughts
- Make picking up your camera a natural response to anxiety
- Find a relaxing space that you visit weekly for photography, such as a nearby lake or woodland where there is a lot of wildlife
- Create a calming space in your house for editing the photos you take
- Print out your favourite photos to display in your home and use them to prompt positive affirmations. For example, "Every time I see this photo, I think of a peaceful place."

It's easy to get lost in creativity, but being intentional about and using it as a mindful activity can also help take the wind out of anxiety's sails.

GO AFTER YOUR LIFE GOALS

Arguably, the ultimate act of self-care is to prioritize going after the life we want. We all have life goals, but these may seem out of reach due to the anxiety that holds us back. By acknowledging our goals and committing to chasing them despite our anxieties, we can start to feel more in control of life and less consumed by worry.

If your goal is to one day write a book, start today by writing the first page. If your goal is to climb a mountain, phone a friend and ask if they would like to go on a small hike this weekend. If your goal is to start a business, write up your business plan this week and seek out feedback from someone you trust.

If you have a dream that you think about a lot, you owe it to yourself to take the first step and see how it goes. Anxiety will always be present in some form or another, but as you learn to manage it more effectively, use your newfound freedom to go after the life you've always wanted.

THE IMPORTANCE OF FEELING ORGANIZED

Anxiety can sometimes arise because of a general sense of disorganization. If you don't have mental clarity on what is coming up in your life, what you need to do, or what information you need to hold inside your mind, things can feel a bit chaotic and lead to anxious thoughts.

Having order in your life – in whatever way works for you – can help you to feel in control, in-the-know, and prepared for anything that's thrown your way. Whether it's a calendar in which to write down your appointments, a diary to keep on top of birthdays and other upcoming events, a journal to make checklists, or some other organizational tool, whatever you use to feel more organized is a positive thing.

Your plans and goals shouldn't be so rigid that they are inflexible, but keeping an eye on the next few days, weeks, months – even year – can help you to mentally arrange what's on the horizon, what you need to do, and what you can delegate. Ultimately, this means that you no longer need to keep the information in your mind and consequently you'll feel lighter.

MESSY BRAIN DUMP

A great first step to organizing a messy mind is to do a brain dump, like we did on page 40. Think of all the things that are cluttering up your brain: unfinished tasks, things you've been meaning to get done for ages, appointments you need to book, projects you're keen to start, people you want to catch up with... write it all down in one giant list so it's no longer burdening your mind and can be found on this page when you need it.

ORGANIZED BRAIN DUMP

Now that you have taken everything out of your brain and written it on the page, categorizing it can help you start to see which areas of your life are causing you the most anxiety, and therefore require the most energy. Look back at your brain dump from the previous page and move each item into one of the categories listed here.

Home	Relationship	Family

Friends	Work/School	Other

By now you should be beginning to notice which parts of your life are causing you the most anxiety. Start giving these areas more attention in order to remove some of the "to-dos" listed above, and eventually you'll feel better about them.

PRIORITIZING SELF-CARE

With everything else going on in our lives, we tend to allow self-care activities to fall to the bottom of our to-do lists, as they seem like the least of our priorities and don't concern anyone except ourselves. Though at the time this probably seems like the best option in order to get through our more time-sensitive tasks, the more we neglect self-care, the more it becomes a "maybe one day" activity rather than a "must do" activity, and the closer we inch towards burnout.

There are many tools within this book for tackling anxiety, but self-care remains a crucial element of our mental well-being, one that we must prioritize, no matter how busy we become in daily life. Here are a few ways in which you can ensure that you prioritize your self-care:

- Don't write your self-care activities on a to-do list, write them on a calendar so there is a date and time attached to them, and treat them like an appointment.
- Start scheduling self-care activities now for the month ahead, and plan everything else around them.
- Decide on your "non-negotiable". What is the one thing each week that can have the most positive impact on your anxiety? Make sure this is always on your calendar, no matter what.
- Let other people know when you'll be busy. Explain that you feel you can be a better colleague/partner/parent/friend/person if you have a little time each week for self-care.

SELF-CARE FOR BUSY SCHEDULES

By now you might be thinking "It's all well and good to say that I should prioritize self-care, but what if I'm already stretched too thin? Where do I find the time?"

Everyone's situation is different, and one person's self-care schedule won't necessarily work for another, especially if they have a stressful job, young children, boisterous pets, a busy family life, lots of friends, caring responsibilities, shift work... the list goes on.

We all have the same 24 hours in the day, but it is undoubtedly difficult for some people to make time for self-care. Prioritizing it may mean that you need to do an audit of your life and find other things in your schedule that can be postponed. For example:

- Could you book a day off work once a quarter?
- Could you delegate organizing the family holiday to someone else this year?
- Could you consider employing a babysitter so that you can enjoy some "you" time?
- Could you hire someone to help with anything on your list that can be outsourced?
- Could you request a new shift pattern at work that better suits your lifestyle?

MICRO SELF-CARE MOMENTS

You can make self-care happen anywhere, even if you're not in your usual environment.

If you have a jam-packed schedule, you may need to think of small ways in which you can bring self-care into the activities you're already doing. This comes back to the idea that you need to make your own joy by finding the fun in life. Review your schedule and find the in-between times when you can do fun or relaxing things in order to de-stress and reduce your anxiety.

Here are a few examples of micro self-care moments you may be able to find in your day:

- Recite an affirmation in the shower each morning
- Do a short meditation while the kids are napping
- Put on an empowering podcast or a feel-good playlist on the drive to work
- Between work meetings, set a 5-minute timer and journal how you're feeling
- Read a book on your train or bus journeys
- While cooking dinner, think of as many reasons as you can to be grateful for your life

SCHEDULE MICRO SELF-CARE MOMENTS

Just as you previously noted down your current and ideal self-care schedules, make a note in the table below of when you might be able to find time for micro self-care moments throughout each day.

	Morning	Afternoon	Evening
MON			
TUES			
WED			
THUR			
FRI			
SAT			
SUN			

In the madness of the moment, you may forget to do these self-care activities, so it's always best to set an alarm or reminder of some sort.

SELF-CARE IS NOT SELFISH

Self-care is, unfortunately, often thought of as a selfish act. It is caring for oneself, which often means putting our own needs in front of the needs of others.

Always remember that **self-care is not selfish**.

By making time for self-care, we can become calmer, more balanced, more logical, more thoughtful and more caring – all-round better human beings for the people around us. Self-care is putting your own oxygen mask on first so that you can help others to do the same. It is prioritizing your health and wellness so you show up as the best version of yourself for the people in your life.

Don't let anyone make you feel guilty for taking time to yourself in order to put your wellness first. If this is what you feel you need to do to tackle symptoms of anxiety, it will ultimately help both you and the people you love.

SELF-CARE PLEDGE

End this chapter by making a pledge to yourself to prioritize self-care. The power of self-care can be transformative and can have such a positive effect on feelings of anxiety, so commit to whatever it is that keeps you feeling well by writing it down. You can use the template below if it helps, or feel free to write out your own from scratch.

I,   , pledge to make

time for self-care activities on a regular basis to help me feel less

                                                    and more

                                                    .

I know that self-care is essential to help me

SUMMARY: THE POWER OF SELF-CARE

You will now understand the importance of self-care for anxiety, and why it's not helpful to allow it to slide further down your to-do list each week. This chapter included a deep dive into:

- What real self-care is (not what it might look like from the outside)
- Why self-kindness and self-compassion are so important
- Physical self-care activities that make a big difference, like eating well and getting enough sleep
- How to create a self-care schedule (even for the busiest people)
- Why healthy boundaries are a form of self-care, and how to set them without losing friends
- The importance of clearing your mind of all the smaller things whirling around in there.

Any time you're feeling stressed or burned out, you can come back to the self-care strategies in this chapter as a reminder to focus on your physical and emotional needs to help reduce feelings of anxiety.

CHAPTER 4:

COPING

STRATEGIES

Anxiety, in one form or another, is an inevitable part of life, and that's OK. You can learn to live with it and what's more, you can learn to thrive with it. The coping strategies in this chapter can help you to:

- Avoid jumping to negative conclusions when triggered
- Feel calmer during stressful life events
- Approach stressful situations with a clear, level head and a logical mind
- Make better decisions under pressure
- Show up as the best version of yourself in all situations

... and much more.

Coping well with anxiety can change your life for the better, so this chapter will show you some effective tools for staying in the present moment, remaining calm and mindful in the face of anxiety triggers, handling your anxiety long term, and celebrating your strengths.

By the end, you will have created your very own Anxiety First-Aid Kit that you can bring out during life's most stressful moments.

GET COMFORTABLE WITH BEING UNCOMFORTABLE

Short-term anxiety typically happens as a response to a specific event or to a decision you must make, and it has an end point in sight. An example might be an exam, which has a clear deadline. Long-term anxiety, on the other hand, is something you live with continually, or something that comes up regularly due to a recurring situation that has no end point. An example might be social anxiety, which will come up each time you must socialize with others.

If you suffer from long-term anxiety, you will benefit from getting comfortable with being uncomfortable. While the easiest solution to social anxiety would be to never engage in any social interaction for the rest of your life, it is not realistic to believe you can always avoid these situations.

We must learn to embrace what scares us if we are to experience all the wonderful things that life has to offer, such as making new friends at social gatherings. By shying away from everything that causes us anxiety, we would live a sad, lonely and uninteresting life. So it's time to embrace the uncomfortable!

WRITE OUT THE
WORST-CASE SCENARIO

How many times have you catastrophized a situation and predicted the absolute worst? When anxiety strikes ahead of a big life event or decision (or something day-to-day that fills you with dread), it's so easy to skip straight to the worst thing that could possibly happen. For example: "If I put my dog into doggy day-care, he will definitely eat something he's not supposed to and get sick" or "My boss has almost certainly called the meeting to fire me."

Chances are that your anxious mind is greatly exaggerating what is likely to occur, so instead of letting the thoughts take root and grow from a tiny sapling of possibility into a giant tree of inevitability, write it all down. Getting thoughts from your brain to the page can help a lot in making you see how overblown your assumptions probably are.

What is the worst-case scenario? What if you turned up to the situation completely unprepared? What if your assumptions about the event were all true? What if you forgot everything you needed to know to get through it? What if everything that could go wrong, did?

In most instances, the worst-case scenario is unlikely to be life-threatening. If it makes you feel better, you can also write down a plan of action in the unlikely event that the worst *does* in fact happen.

WHEN LIFE GIVES
YOU LEMONS,
MAKE LEMONADE

WORST. DAY. EVER.

The worst-case scenario is almost never what happens in reality. Our brains tend to catastrophize, so use the space below to let it all out. Bring to mind what you get anxious about most and then imagine the worst version of how it could play out.

Then, underneath this, write a mini plan of action for how you would handle it if the worst-case scenario *did* actually occur.

The worst-case scenario would be

If this happens, I will

WRITE OUT THE
BEST-CASE SCENARIO

Why is it that we favour imagining the worst over imagining the best? Anxiety favours the negative, so it's not often that we let ourselves daydream about the possibility of the best-case scenario... but what if we did?

As we know, writing down thoughts can help us process them, so let your creativity run wild and figure out what could go *right*.

What is the best-case scenario? What if you were praised for your genius, your comedy, your looks, or something else that might make you feel great? What if you met an amazing new friend at the event? What if you have the best day of your life today? What if everything that can go right, *does* go right?

Imagining things in this way can not only make you feel better about what is coming up, but it can also help you to manifest the positive situation you seek. For example, if you were to believe that your new best friend will be at a party you are nervous about attending, you may be more likely to go, and therefore more open to chatting to people and making friends.

BEST. DAY. EVER!

Anxiety doesn't tend to favour the best-case scenario since it clouds the mind with all the possible negative outcomes. So, use the space below to imagine the best outcome for an upcoming event or situation. It can be a whole day, an afternoon, an evening, or even a future social event in your calendar. By imagining it, you can make it possible!

The best-case scenario will be

WHAT WOULD HAPPEN IF...?

A great exercise for recognizing all the amazing things that could happen if anxiety wasn't in your way is to start by visualizing both versions of your life.

Write a few sentences in answer to the following questions:

1. What would happen if I let my anxiety win, and gave in to all of its demands? Where would I be in ten years' time?

2. What would happen if I took steps to tackle my anxiety, and it stopped having such a tight grip on me? Where would I be in ten years' time?

Which version of your life would you like to see come to fruition? If you answered version two, it's time to discover some more of the coping strategies that will help make it happen.

IN THE MOMENT:
DEALING WITH SHORT-TERM ANXIETY

For short-term anxiety, your medicine cabinet of self-care principles and mind-quieting exercises will come in handy. You can use strategies from the previous chapters to act as circuit breakers when short-term stress is affecting you. Here is a reminder of the tools at your disposal, and why they are useful:

Spending time outdoors

Practising breathwork or meditation

Getting plenty of rest and adequate sleep

Journalling

Eating a balanced diet

Practising gratitude

Drinking plenty of water

Spending time with people who uplift you

Spending less time on social media

Becoming more organized in daily life

Setting healthy boundaries

Expressing your feelings through creativity

Moving your body

Remember, most of these strategies can be used anywhere and don't cost money. Whether you need to do them at home in private, or silently at your workstation, you're sure to find a practice that works for you.

DON'T BE AFRAID
TO TAKE A BREATHER

Sometimes anxiety can be overwhelming, and when this happens, you may want to change your environment. Just as a holiday can provide a new perspective on home life, or a day off from work can allow the brain to mull over problems and solutions, a change in environment may also be helpful if anxiety is becoming overwhelming.

Not every situation will be something you can easily walk away from (for example, walking away in the middle of a singing performance would not be advisable!). However, if circumstances allow, take a few minutes away from the situation to gather your thoughts, take some deep breaths, and brainstorm the best way to handle what's in front of you.

If you're at a party, excuse yourself for a minute in order to recharge for the next conversation.

If the drive to work is stressful, pull over for a minute to regain a feeling of control and calm.

If your colleagues are causing problems, take a half-day off to reset.

Important: If anxiety overwhelms you to the extent that you have panic attacks, lose certain physical functions, or feel you may hurt yourself or someone else, you should seek immediate medical assistance and work with a professional until you feel better.

INSTANT STRESS BUSTERS

When your anxiety balloon blows up so much that you know it's going to pop, it's time to bust that stress. Here are a few stress-busting tactics to use when anxiety flares up, with a few blank spaces to add your own.

Do some vigorous exercise to move your body and break a sweat

Put on your favourite song and dance like no one is watching you

Do a fun activity you have never tried before

Go for a long walk in nature

Take ten slow, deep breaths

Call a trusted friend and vent what's on your mind

Book a day off work

FORGET THE FUTURE

In almost all scenarios, anxiety comes from worrying about what will happen in the future, or ruminating on what has happened in the past. Learning to live in the present moment and to be mindful of what is going on around you is a great way to say goodbye to anxiety.

Although the future can be influenced by our actions (such as studying for an upcoming exam or buying a new outfit to improve confidence at a social event), it cannot be predicted. Spending so much time worrying about the future is therefore not only a waste of time, it also means that we miss what's going on around us in the present.

Similarly, the past has already happened, and although we can learn from what we might consider to be past mistakes, we can't change it. So spending time ruminating on the past is not only a waste of time, again it leads us to miss what's going on in the present. Are you starting to see a pattern here?

Pulling your attention back to the present moment is a great way to release anxiety quickly, and there are a number of ways you can do this.

FIND FIVE THINGS

One exercise that can be incredibly useful for bringing yourself back to the present moment is to find five things around you: one you can see, one you can hear, once you can touch, one you can smell, and one you can taste. Try it to calm any anxiety flare-ups:

Right now, I can see

I can hear

I can feel

I can smell

I can taste

... AND RELAAAAAX

This exercise is a great one that can be done almost anywhere. If you feel tense, start to scan your body and work on relaxing each individual muscle one by one. You can start from your feet or from your head, and don't pay attention to how long it takes. By the end of the exercise, you should feel calmer, looser, and have fewer anxious thoughts.

Try this while sitting in a chair:

Start by going through each muscle in your head...

- Are you frowning?
- Are you clenching your jaw?
- Do you feel any tension in your face?

Move down your neck to your shoulders...

- Are they hunched over?
- Could you drop your shoulders more?
- Is there any tension in your chest or back?

Move down your torso...

- Are you squeezing your tummy muscles?
- Is your back arched or stiff?

Move down your legs...

- Are your thighs fully relaxed?
- How about your calf muscles?
- Are each of your toes relaxed?

You may do a faster version or take even more time to go through every single muscle in your body. Either way, use this as a handy tool whenever you feel tense.

BACK TO THE PRESENT

Another great way to bring your attention back to the present moment is to journal. Sit in a comfortable place and write what is going on around you, and what your life is like right now. Try to write your thoughts as easily as they enter your mind. This can be about the present moment while journalling, or it could be about this particular day or stage of your life – whatever is most relevant to the anxieties you're experiencing.

THINK OUTSIDE THE BOX

Often the best and quickest way to ease anxious thoughts is to go in search of a solution to whatever problem you're facing. This may seem obvious, but it can be surprising how easy it is for rumination and worry to take over, and we forget that there could be a creative solution to the problem. For example:

Anxiety: You can't stop worrying about an upcoming sales pitch.

Problem: You feel unprepared and inexperienced.

Possible solution: You could ask a colleague with experience to help you prepare so you feel more confident.

Anxiety: You think you might have upset your friend last time you saw them, but you're not sure how they feel about the interaction.

Problem: You feel embarrassed and ashamed.

Possible solution: You could call and ask them, and be prepared to apologize in order to make you both feel better.

Sometimes anxiety arises from situations we have no control over, but at other times, a little out-of-the-box problem-solving can make you feel instantly better. Often the solution is surprisingly simple, even if it feels uncomfortable.

BECOME A PROBLEM-SOLVER

Time to solve some problems of your own! Go back through the previous exercises and see what problems in your life you have written down. Choose two you have control over, that have the potential to be eliminated with a simple step, just like the examples on the previous page. This might mean delegating a task to someone else, rescheduling an event, buying an item, or something else.

Anxiety 1

I'm worried about

This worry started because

One possible solution could be

My next action step is

Anxiety 2

I'm worried about

This worry started because

One possible solution could be

My next action step is

SURF THE ANXIETY WAVE

Solutions can be discovered when we least expect them, but in some cases, our anxieties are based on situations that either can't be changed or can't be changed by us. In these cases, we must learn to surf.

Anxiety tends to come in waves. As one passes, another one starts to swell underneath, building in intensity until it reaches breaking point on the surface. Sometimes you'll need to catch the wave and surf it until you feel better about the situation, and other times you'll simply need to wait until the source of your anxiety passes. In any case, remember that it will always pass.

Affirmation:

No matter how rough the seas, I can surf the waves of anxiety and gently float to the shore.

You could trace this line with your finger or draw waves to remind yourself to surf the waves of anxiety.

ANXIETY IS
SOMETHING THAT
IS PART OF ME
BUT IT'S NOT
WHO I AM.

_____

Emma Stone

PHONE A FRIEND

If a solution to a problem doesn't come to mind, sometimes talking about it can help process it, put it into context, gather outside opinions, or hear new perspectives that lead to solutions. As we learned on page 68, talking about our anxieties can not only help us release them, it can give us access to someone else's point of view, which could be entirely different to our own and therefore hold the solution we're looking for.

Ask yourself if there is someone in your life who would be best placed to give you some helpful advice on a particular subject. This could be your partner, a family member, a friend, a colleague at work (if appropriate), or someone else in your life who you trust with your feelings. Try to see them in person for a catch-up or call them on the phone.

You may want to specify whether you are:

A. Telling them about your anxieties in the hopes that they can offer advice and a different perspective, or

B. Telling them to get feelings off your chest, but are not interested in their input or suggestions for solutions.

C. Either is fine, and you can request the latter in a friendly way, so they know what you need from the discussion. Remember, the boundaries are up to you.

VISUALIZATION

Visualization is a handy coping strategy that can help you to reduce anxiety through imagining an ideal scenario or the desired outcome of a situation. By picturing yourself tackling and successfully navigating an upcoming challenge with ease, you can begin to calm your brain and see a future where the source of your anxiety is resolved. If you can see it in your mind's eye, you can imagine achieving it – and if you can achieve it in your mind, you can achieve it in real life too.

Visualization can:

- Create a relaxation response
- Help you reach a constructive solution to whatever is causing your anxiety
- Promote a sense of control over your thoughts and emotions
- Distract you from your anxious thoughts for a while
- Be a fun exercise that uses your imagination

You could write your visualizations in a journal, close your eyes and picture it all silently in your mind, or describe it out loud to a friend: whatever you feel works best for you.

VISUALIZE: HOW DO YOU FEEL?

Try this exercise. Visualize your life several years from now and picture your perfect day. Use the space below to write down exactly how you would feel as you go about your best day in your anxiety-free life. Be as specific as you like but focus on how you feel.

VISUALIZE: HOW DO YOU LOOK TO THE OUTSIDE WORLD?

Now, visualize your life once more several years from now. It's that same perfect day, and this time you can use the space below to write down exactly what other people would see if they passed you on the street. What does the anxiety-free version of you look like?

LEARN TO INTERRUPT THOUGHTS

When beginning to tackle your anxiety, learn to throw politeness out of the window! Don't wait for anxiety to finish its negative thought before you jump in to interrupt it – doing so allows anxious thoughts to take root and grow.

These thoughts tend to follow a pattern of escalating negativity. Shutting them down early can help you regain control of your mind and bring your attention back to the reality of the situation.

When interrupting an anxious thought, try to acknowledge its presence without judgement and immediately challenge it:

"Is that true? Where did I get this information from? Am I focusing on the negative and discounting the positive? Do I have any evidence that this is the case?"

By reframing and re-evaluating your anxious thoughts, you can start to view them from a more rational standpoint, and work to replace them with balanced, more evidence-based alternatives. The more we do this, the better we become at tackling anxiety.

PUSH PAST ANXIETY

Why do we bother pushing past the feeling of anxiety in the first place? Why can't we just give in to its demands? Life would be easier that way... right?

If you are reading this book, you probably already know why it's important to push past anxiety.

Beyond the discomfort of anxiety lies everything we want out of life. We go on dates despite our anxiety because we want a connection. We present in big meetings despite our anxiety because we want to progress in our career. We force ourselves to travel despite our anxiety because we want to experience new places.

There are so many reasons to give in to anxiety, but there are a million more reasons to feel the fear but continue anyway. Pushing past anxiety is how we learn new things, have new experiences, meet new people, go to new places, and more.

WHAT IS THE COMFORT ZONE?

Your comfort zone is where you are most comfortable, settled and confident. It is not necessarily a physical place. The comfort zone is an imaginary personal boundary outside of which exists everything you are *un*comfortable doing or experiencing.

For example, here is what the comfort zone might look like for someone with social anxiety:

Everyone has their own comfort zone, usually based on past experiences and whatever causes them anxiety. For one person, skydiving may be within their comfort zone, while talking to members of the opposite sex may be outside it. For another, the opposite may be true.

YOUR COMFORT ZONE

Discovering what is inside and outside your comfort zone can help you make clearer boundaries for yourself. Use the diagram below to write some things that spring to mind.

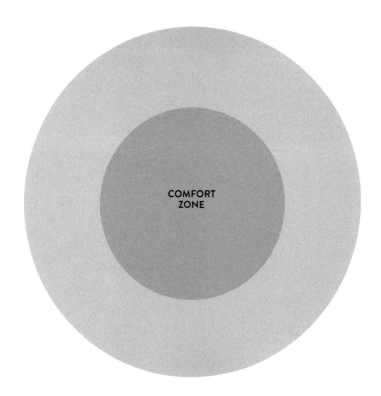

COMFORT
ZONE

EXPAND YOUR COMFORT ZONE

We know it's important to expand our comfort zone, but how do we begin to do this? Some people prefer to jump in at the deep end, while others (in what is usually the recommended course) take baby steps to slowly expand their comfort zone. Here are examples of both options.

The Deep End:

Anxiety: Driving to a new place.

Underlying fear: I will get into an accident.

Expanding the comfort zone: Choose a place far away on the map, get in the car and drive.

Baby Steps:

Anxiety: Driving to a new place.

Underlying fear: I will get into an accident.

Expanding the comfort zone: Today, choose a place just a little further on from where you usually drive to, and go there. Tomorrow, choose somewhere a little further still, and continue this cycle until you begin to feel more confident behind the wheel.

Both options are useful, but if the underlying fear is about getting into an accident then perhaps option two is best. This will allow you to feel confident for the majority of the drive and add a little more to the journey each time so that you're learning in smaller increments rather than in smaller increments.

CREATE YOUR SUPPORT NETWORK

We don't need to manage our anxiety alone. Everyone can develop a support network to help them through tough situations and provide them with an outside perspective. Chances are you already have support around you, but if you have never really thought about it, it can be helpful to make a list of who is in your support network, and what you might call on them for.

Perhaps one of your parents is really good with money and accounting and could be the best person to talk to about financial anxiety. Or maybe you know another parent at your child's school who is always understanding and non-judgemental, and could be a great person to chat to about parental anxieties. Or it could be that one of your friends gives great life advice and can support you with a generally positive outlook whenever you need it.

Think about the people in your life who may be able to help you with specific things, and always remember that help should be a two-way street. Invest in your relationship by making sure that they know you are also there to lend a listening ear or offer some advice if they ever need it.

_____'S SUPPORT NETWORK

It's time to think about who you could have in your own support network. For each important area of your life, write down one person you can call on. Consider who has experience in that area, who tends to give the best advice, and who would be open to discussing your anxious thoughts.

ANXIETY FIRST-AID KIT: WHAT IS IT?

Just like a regular first-aid kit that you would bring out of the cupboard if you had an accident, your Anxiety First-Aid Kit is filled with metaphorical medicines that can be opened any time anxiety starts to flare up. It's your box of tricks, or the tool belt that's always attached to you: you just need to remember it's there.

It's important to make your own Anxiety First-Aid Kit, because each person has completely different anxieties, triggers, circumstances, social networks, and so on. You can make an entirely personalized kit that's just for you, based on the coping strategies you know work for you.

This could be some physical movement to release any pent-up energy or a mindfulness exercise to bring you back to the present moment. It could be a chat with a specific person in your support network, a mindset switch to help you surf the wave of anxiety, or something else that makes you instantly feel better.

ANXIETY FIRST-AID KIT: BRAINSTORM

Before you make your official Anxiety First-Aid Kit, brainstorm the tools and strategies from this book and beyond that could be useful. Get creative and list what you think could help to curb your anxiety, what you'd like to try for the first time, and what sparks your interest. This could include a 15-minute meditation, a nightly gratitude journal, a call to someone in your support network once a week, an affirmation about your boundaries, sticking to a weekly step count, or something else.

_____'S ANXIETY FIRST-AID KIT

Armed with your brainstorm list, it's now time to start your very own Anxiety First-Aid Kit. Try to think of five things that would be useful to you in an anxious situation and write them in the spaces below.

I tend to get anxious when

When I feel this way, I know I can

I try to remember

I tend to think   , but I can reframe this

thought to

The most important thing I do for my mental health is

Come back to this page any time you're experiencing anxiety and want some simple tips for stopping it in its tracks.

Remember: write Post-it notes to keep the advice in mind, or take a picture of the page and add it to your phone background – whatever you need to do to remember that your Anxiety First-Aid Kit is there any time you need it.

SUMMARY: COPING STRATEGIES

You will now have tried quite a few potential coping strategies to calm anxiety in a way that works specifically for you, your goals, your lifestyle and more. This chapter included a deep dive into:

- How to become comfortable with being uncomfortable, and why it's helpful to imagine both the worst- and best-case scenarios
- Strategies that can pull you back to the present moment when your mind is rushing at 100 miles an hour
- The difference between sources of anxiety you can take action on, and sources of anxiety that you can't change
- What lies on the other side of anxiety and why it's important to push past it
- What your comfort zone is and how to begin to expand it over time
- Creating your own Anxiety First-Aid Kit to use during life's most stressful, anxious moments.

The coping strategies in this chapter and throughout this book can be used any time an anxiety flare-up occurs, but you can also start to incorporate some of them into daily life as a preventative measure. Every day can begin in a calm, carefree and confident way.

TODAY, I
SAY GOODBYE
TO ANXIETY,
AND HELLO
TO POSSIBILITY

CONCLUSION

Addressing your anxiety won't always be easy, but can be an incredibly liberating process. The more positive change you begin to feel, the more you'll want to continue on your journey and uncover even more confidence in yourself.

The advice in this book offers a foundation on which you can build a life with less anxiety and more ease. By understanding the root cause of your own anxiety, and using a helpful set of tools to manage it day-to-day, you can feel reassured that you have everything you need to tackle any situation, no matter how challenging.

Whether you're just getting started on your journey to better understand your mind, or are looking for further resources to stop anxiety in its tracks, these coping strategies can be referred back to in any circumstance.

Kudos on completing this crash course in fixing your anxiety! The advice in this book, alongside your positive attitude and desire to live a more fulfilling life, will stand you in good stead for the journey ahead. Your anxiety does not define who you are, and you can do amazing things if you learn to harness it in the right way. Best of luck!

RESOURCES

In addition to the advice throughout this book, here are some sources that may provide further support and guidance as you learn to manage your anxiety.

Websites

www.mind.org.uk

Mental health charity Mind provides lots of information about specific mental health concerns on their website, including anxiety.

www.happiful.com

Happiful magazine is all about mental health, and they have a tag on their website that will filter all articles on the subject of anxiety to learn more – fascinating stuff!

www.headspace.com

The Headspace app is a great meditation tool for practising mindfulness, either during an anxiety flare-up or as a preventative measure.

Podcasts

Happy Place

On this podcast, broadcaster Fearne Cotton discusses all things happiness with inspiring guests, and anxiety is a regular topic.

Ten Percent Happier

Author and journalist Dan Harris is known for having once had a panic attack on live television. He eventually found meditation, wrote a bestselling book, and now hosts his own podcast.

Social Anxiety Solutions

Host Sebastiaan van der Schrier is a recovered social anxiety sufferer and helps people who continue to suffer with social anxiety.

Books

The Anxiety Workbook: Practical Tips and Guided Exercises to Help You Overcome Anxiety, Anna Barnes (2022)

Unwinding Anxiety: Train Your Brain to Heal Your Mind, Judson Brewer (2021)

The Anxiety Solution: A Quieter Mind, a Calmer You, Chloe Brotheridge (2017)

How to Stop Overthinking: The 7-Step Plan to Control and Eliminate Negative Thoughts, Declutter Your Mind and Start Thinking Positively in 5 Minutes or Less, Chase Hill and Scott Sharp (2019)

How to Understand and Deal with Social Anxiety, Mita Mistry (2022)

Breath: The New Science of a Lost Art, James Nestor (2021)

No More Worries! Outsmart Anxiety and Be Positively You, Poppy O'Neill (2021)

Overcoming Overthinking: The Complete Guide to Calm Your Mind by Conquering Anxiety, Sleeplessness, Indecision, and Negative Thoughts, Kirk Teachout (2023)

THE CONFIDENCE FIX

Empowering Exercises to Build Your Self-Esteem

Debbi Marco

Paperback

ISBN: 978-1-83799-306-2

Embrace your inner confidence and unleash your full potential with this simple guide to boosting your self-esteem.

Confidence isn't something we are born with, but instead is a skill that can be learned and developed over time. Filled with inspiring statements and practical activities, *The Confidence Fix* is a gentle and encouraging guide on how to grow your self-assurance.

By working through the prompts and exercises in this workbook, you will be able to find your inner strength, develop your resilience and build your self-belief. With inspirational quotes and space for personal reflections, this beautiful and powerful workbook is here to encourage daily self-care and personal growth.